D0344917

The Importance of Being Funny

PRAISE FOR *THE IMPORTANCE OF BEING FUNNY*

"I've known Al Gini since I was five years old. I always thought of him as the hilarious kook who lived down the street. Until I read this excellent book, I had no idea that he was, in fact, a gainfully employed, productive member of our society. This book is so insightful, I highly recommend it. We need more Al Ginis in our lives." —**Thomas Lennon**, of Comedy Central's *Reno 911* and CBS's *The Odd Couple*; coauthor of the *Night at the Museum* movies

"I have been the victim of some of Gini's early research for this book, being one of his unsuspecting students many years ago. I had intended to attend and listen to boring lectures about dry philosophy subjects. But he'd interject humor and therefore make it nearly impossible to forget the lessons. [Shaking fist at sky . . .] Damn you, Gini!" —**David Pasquesi**, Chicago's Second City, HBO's *Veep*, Improviser of the Year by Chicago Improv Festival

"Gini gives us a careful examination of comedy and its central importance in our lives, from the classroom to the boardroom to the bedroom, managing to extricate precisely where, why, and how something can be funny without ever spoiling the good time with pedantic antics. I learned and LOL'ed simultaneously." —**Zach Freeman**, *Chicago Tribune* comedy critic

"*The Importance of Being Funny* is both important and funny. The French existentialist Albert Camus said that life is absurd. Gini agrees and argues that, in order to live it well, we need to embrace the absurdity. Laughter isn't just the best medicine but also the very stuff of life." —**Steven Gimbel**, Gettysburg College

"Gini attempts to recover the joyfulness of humor by deriving it from the best—and most demanding—material of all: the baffling contours of everyday experiences and our uproariously futile attempts to make complete sense of life. Humor, in Gini's hands, is sometimes homey, mostly honest, and ultimately humane. A timely and entertaining offering!" —**Gregory Wolcott**, Saint Mary's College of California

The Importance of Being Funny

Why We Need More Jokes in Our Lives

AL GINI

ROWMAN & LITTLEFIELD
Lanham • Boulder • New York • London

Published by Rowman & Littlefield
A wholly owned subsidiary of The Rowman & Littlefield Publishing Group, Inc.
4501 Forbes Boulevard, Suite 200, Lanham, Maryland 20706
www.rowman.com

Unit A, Whitacre Mews, 26-34 Stannary Street, London SE11 4AB

Distributed by NATIONAL BOOK NETWORK

Copyright © 2017 Rowman & Littlefield

All rights reserved. No part of this book may be reproduced in any form or by any electronic or mechanical means, including information storage and retrieval systems, without written permission from the publisher, except by a reviewer who may quote passages in a review.

Library of Congress Cataloging-in-Publication Data Available

ISBN 9781442281769 (cloth : alk. paper)
ISBN 9781442281776 (electronic)

♾️™ The paper used in this publication meets the minimum requirements of American National Standard for Information Sciences—Permanence of Paper for Printed Library Materials, ANSI/NISO Z39.48-1992.

Printed in the United States of America

To my Uncle Joe, who made me laugh, and to
Ted Cohen, who taught me about laughter.
I am forever grateful!

There are three things that are real: God, human folly, and laughter. The first two are beyond our comprehension. So we must do what we can with the third.

—JOHN F. KENNEDY

Contents

Acknowledgments ix

Prologue xi

Chapter 1: A Brief, Highly Selective, and Somewhat Fallacious History of Humor and Joke Telling 1

Chapter 2: How Do You Make Funny? So, What's a Joke?. 19

Chapter 3: Comedy and Coping with Reality 37

Chapter 4: Dirty Jokes, Tasteless Jokes, Ethnic Jokes 57

Chapter 5: A Conversation with a Colleague about Humor and Ethics 85

Chapter 6: Philogagging: Humor in the Classroom and Beyond 101

Epilogue 113

Notes 119

Suggested Readings/Humor and Comedy. 131

Index. 137

About the Author. 141

ACKNOWLEDGMENTS

Without the help and support of Ross Miller, Taiwo Adefiyiju, Rebeca Daniels, Jamison Stoltz, Sherry Gini, Carla Gini, Ron Green, Rachel Weaver, Jason Smith, and Jon Sisk, this book would only exist as a figment of my imagination. Many thanks to you all.

PROLOGUE

Somewhere along the line, we've forgotten the true purpose of humor: to help people cope with the fears and horrors of the world.

—KEEGAN-MICHAEL KEY AND JORDAN PEELE

I have been lucky enough to have had a very special person in my life—my Uncle Joe. Every time I saw him he would put his arms around me and whisper in my ear, "Did you hear the one about . . . ?" And then he would tell me a joke. Until the week of his death, Uncle Joe never failed to greet me in this way, and only rarely did he ever repeat himself. On one occasion, in my teens, when I was feeling somewhat rebellious and somehow embarrassed by this tradition, I abruptly pulled away from him and asked why he was always telling me jokes. Uncle Joe took a step back, smiled at me, and said, "Because I love you, *stupido*! If I didn't love you, why would I want to make you happy? Why would I want to make you laugh? Listen to me: a joke is a gift and a weapon that we can use against reality. Jokes aren't always enough, but they can help. Just remember, kid—there's never too much love or laughter in life. *Capisci*?"

Mel Brooks, my uncle's favorite comedic mind, believes that we need humor—we need jokes in our lives because otherwise our "collective lamentations" about the trials and tribulations of the world would be unbearable. That's why, says

Brooks, for every ten people God creates, he designs one to be a comic to entertain and distract the others. We need jokes, Brooks argues, as "a defense against the universe." We need humor to fight off our fear of living. Joke telling is an attempt to keep at a distance our fear of the unknown, the unanswerable, and the unacceptable. For Brooks and my Uncle Joe, jokes make life endurable and worthwhile.[1]

By the way, long before I graduated to Uncle Joe's more "mature" mirth making (he did have a rather naughty side), I had a favorite joke that I begged him to tell me again and again.

Dog for Sale

A guy spots a sign outside of a house that reads "Talking Dog for Sale."

Intrigued, he knocks on the door and asks the owner if he can see the dog.

"So, what have you done with your life?" he asks the dog.

"I've led a very full life," says the dog. "I've lived in the Alps rescuing avalanche victims. I was in the army for eight years. And now I spend my days reading to the residents of a local retirement home."

The guy is flabbergasted. He turns and asks the dog's owner, "Why on earth would you want to get rid of such an incredible dog like that?"

The owner looks at the potential buyer with disgust and replies, "Because he's a damn liar! He never did any of that!"

Following my Uncle Joe's lead, I want to argue that comedy, humor, and, more specifically, joke telling are a means of dealing with the everyday problems of life as well as many of the more elusive and mysterious questions of existence. Humor can act as both a sword and a shield to defend and protect us against life. Humor can, at times, illuminate (if not completely explain) some of the irresoluble problems and mysterious that all of us face. And, if all else fails, humor, at the very least, can hold off our fear of the unanswerable and the unacceptable.

On the last week of his politically significant and culturally altering comedy program, *The Daily Show*, Jon Stewart elegantly encapsulated the time-honored role and purpose of jesters, fools, comedy, comics, and joke telling: "Jokes are a narrative that helps us negotiate reality." Sex keeps us alive and kicking. Intellect gives us art and science. Humor makes life bearable and worthwhile. At least sometimes!

I love jokes. Jokes, good jokes (and even a few bad jokes), are a pleasant distraction. They are a time-out. They offer a moment of reprieve. They are a safety value. They can disarm a moment. They are a weapon against the assault of reality. And, lest we forget, jokes are also simply foolish fun. But they are often less foolish than meets the eye. Case in point: Abraham Lincoln.

Lincoln's presidency was fraught with trauma and turmoil. To begin with, he was seemingly the least-credentialed, most ill-prepared person to ever hold the office. Although he had been in the Illinois legislature for a number of terms, he had only served one term as a US congressman, and he had no experience whatsoever in executive management or military leadership. His fifteen predecessors included victorious generals, vice presidents, secretaries of state, and veteran members of Congress. To make matters worse, even before he took the oath of office, seven Southern states had seceded from the Union, Fort Sumter in South Carolina was under siege, and there was no army group protecting Washington, DC. To add insult to injury, Lincoln was also the butt of humiliating and dehumanizing political cartoons and vicious editorials. According to noted Lincoln scholar William Lee Miller, many Americans, from both the North and the South, felt that Lincoln was not a man equal to the hour.[2]

Lincoln endured and succeeded in his presidency due to a combination of hard work, a shrewd and determined political mind, and a strong sense of humor. Every chance he could, Lincoln sought relief in joke telling, reading satirical essays, and going to plays. According to Doris Kearns Goodwin, Pulitzer Prize–winning American historian, Lincoln's love of theater and his desperate need to find downtime and comfort lead him to attend more than one hundred theatrical performances during his four-plus years as president.[3]

Lincoln saw humor as an essential weapon against distress. It was, for him, a delightful distraction and a coping mechanism that allowed him at least temporary relief from the burdens of his office. He especially loved jokes. He loved telling jokes. And he loved jokes about himself. Here's his favorite:

Two Quaker women were talking about who would win the war—President Lincoln for the United States or Jefferson Davis, who was president of the Southern rebel states.

FIRST QUAKER WOMAN: I think Jefferson Davis will win.

SECOND QUAKER WOMAN: Why does thee thinks so?

FIRST QUAKER WOMAN: Because he is a praying man.

SECOND QUAKER WOMAN: Abraham Lincoln is a praying man too.

FIRST QUAKER WOMAN: Yes, but the Lord will think Abraham is joking.[4]

Jokes, satirical writers, and plays allowed Lincoln to transcend the violence and destruction of the bloody Civil War, the death of his son Willie, and the crushing responsibilities of being president. A good story or joke, Lincoln said, "has the same effect on me that I think a good square drink of whiskey has to the old roper [a craftsman who makes ropes]. It puts new life into me . . . good for both the mental and physical digestions."[5] And he also often said, "If it were not for these stories—jokes—jests, I should die; they give vent—are the vents of my moods and gloom."[6] Like Mark Twain, the nineteenth-century American humorist, Lincoln was convinced that against reality "the human race has only one really effective weapon, and this is laughter."[7] Or, as another iconic American cultural critic and philosopher, Joan Rivers, put it, "If you can laugh at it, you can live with it."[8]

Joke telling offers us a way to deal with some of the unavoidable absurdities, complexities, and paradoxes of life. When we laugh at one of life's mysteries, cruelties, or horrors, we diminish—if only temporarily—its terror in our imagination. Joke telling offers us a window into the unknowable and the irresolvable. Jokes about sex, marriage, children, money, illness, death, religion, and God may not provide definitive answers, but they can alleviate some of our fears, afford comfort and distraction, and maybe, just maybe, offer us some perspective, some illumination in regard to these fundamentally irresolvable and yet unavoidable issues. Jokes allow us to disarm reality and not be defeated by it.

Here are two jokes to whet your appetite. The first touches on the Big Three of Jokedom: Marriage, Sex, and Death. The second is one of my all-time favorites on organized religion and its complexities and nuances.

Mario and Maria

Mario visits his doctor for a routine examination and gets the devastating news that he is mortally ill, with no treatment possible, and that he will die within a day. He goes home, tells his wife, Maria, and, after they have absorbed the shock of the terrible news, Mario says to Maria, "Maria, I know our marriage has not been perfect, but since this is my last night can we just overlook all of our problems? Please, Maria, can we just go to bed and fool around one last time?"

"*Ma*, sure," says Maria. And so they do.

Later, at about 1 a.m., Mario wakes up, prods Maria, and asks, "Do you think we could do it again?"

"Certainly, Mario; it's your last night." And so they do it again.

At 3 a.m., Mario is awake, and again he asks Maria for her attentions.

"For God's sake, Mario, enough already! Give me a break! This is easy for you! You don't have to get up in the morning!"

An Ecumenical Moment

A Lutheran pastor is asleep one night when the phone rings. The fire department is calling to say that someone is about to jump off a roof. The pastor throws on his clothes, jumps in his car, and races to the scene. When he arrives, a firefighter points to the man on his roof.

"Don't jump!" yells the pastor.

"Well, I'm going to," says the man. "I've got nothing to live for!"

The pastor asks, "What about your family?"

And the man says, "I've got none!"

The pastor asks, "What about your friends?"

The man says, "I've got none!"

The pastor pauses for a long while and then says, "Well, I'm sure we could be friends. I'll bet we have a lot in common."

"I doubt it," says the man on the roof.

The pastor thinks. "Well, do you believe in God?"

"Yes," says the man.

"See?" says the pastor. "We have that in common! Are you a Christian?"

"Yes," says the man.

"So am I!" says the pastor, delighted. "Are you Lutheran by any chance?"

"Yes, I am," he says.

"I'm a Lutheran pastor!" says the pastor. "We have so much in common!" Then he pauses and asks, "Which branch—Missouri Synod or Evangelical Lutheran?"

"Evangelical Lutheran," says the man.

Then the pastor says, "In that case, jump, you damn heretic!"[9]

This book is not a complete history or investigation of humor, because, as has been said, studying humor is like studying sex or subatomic particles: the more you analyze it, the more elusive it becomes. In particular, I want to focus on jokes and joke telling as well as the people who tell jokes. Consequently, I will not be delving into the slapstick antics of the Three Stooges or the stereotypical pratfalls of circus clowns. Nor will I be analyzing such libidinous limericks as "There once was a man from Nantucket . . ." I also will not be pondering the comic value of puns or poems or even the exquisite comedic quatrains of Dorothy Parker:

I like to drink a Martini

But only two at the most.

Three, I'm under the table;

Four, I'm under the host.[10]

I shall eschew any and all "Yogi-isms" (Yogi Berra was a baseball player on the New York Yankees for nineteen years and was a master of malapropisms): "We made too many wrong mistakes." "Half the lies they tell about me aren't true." And "It's like déjà vu all over again." I will also overlook the classical theatrics of commedia dell'arte, the whole genre of comic novels, essays, TV sitcoms, and plays, as well as the modern American cultural icon of comedy—*Saturday Night Live*.

The title of this text, *The Importance of Being Funny*, is an intentional play on Oscar Wilde's most famous theatrical creation, from 1885, *The Importance of Being Earnest*. Wilde's title suggests that it is important to be earnest, to be honest, and sincere, even if, *ironically*, none of the characters in his play is, in fact, earnest or sincere. I, on the other hand, am not being ironic. I literally mean that it is important, and perhaps even critically necessary, to have a sense of humor, to be funny, to tell or be responsive to jokes in our lives. As Wilde himself pointed out in his very first play, *Vera; or, The Nihilists*, "Life is too important a thing ever to [always and only] talk seriously about it."

All too often we cannot change or control the facts of life or the course of our fate, but we can control our attitude in regard to the particular facts of our fate. For me, humor and joke telling describe the *attitude* I choose to face the irrelevant, the tragic, the absurd, and the overwhelming matters of life that are beyond my control and comprehension. Of course, there is a caveat: humor is not a cure for life, but it can be a helpful anesthesia. I am convinced that laughter both demonstrates and reinforces our humanity, encourages hope, and allows us to endure with dignity. Humor or joke telling may not be able to offer definitive answers, but it can arrest and detox our uncertainty. Both seriousness and silliness are critical parts of a meaningful life.

Before I present a brief synopsis of the individual chapters, allow me to offer a few caveats. To begin with, I recognize that any analysis of humor can prove to be all too humorless, even distasteful, on at least two counts. First, the danger in studying comedy is analogous to watching someone make sausage: witnessing its creation often makes the final product less than appetizing, and the whole experience can leave a funny (pun intended!) and unsatisfying taste in your mouth. Second, in putting comedy under close scrutiny, Heisenberg's uncertainty principle comes into play. That principle avers that the more you observe a thing, the more you alter it, change it, modify it. Comedy dies quickly under a microscope. Cool reflection can ruin the pristine spontaneity, timing, and energy of an unadulterated comic experience. And so, to partially compensate for this failing, I have inserted as many jokes into the text as good taste—or, for that matter, bad taste—will allow. The jokes that I use in this text come from a collection of jokes that I have put together over the last twenty years. One of the founding fathers of TV comedy, Milton Berle, once said, "I only tell great jokes because I only steal from the best." None of the jokes cited here is stolen. The vast majority of them have been used, in one version or another, by generations of comedians, and therefore I very rarely attribute them to any one particular comic. Jokes that have been crafted by comedians for specific stand-up routines have, of course, here been given proper credit or attribution.

CHAPTER 1: A BRIEF, HIGHLY SELECTIVE, AND SOMEWHAT FALLACIOUS HISTORY OF HUMOR AND JOKE TELLING

Relax! This is not a formal academic analysis of the origins of humor in our development as a species. Believe me, that wouldn't be any fun at all! I simply want to sketch out some of the more salient moments in the evolution of humor and joke telling. For example, historians tell us that joke telling can be traced back to early Egyptian and biblical times. We also know that the Greeks and the Romans published joke collections. In the Middle Ages, joke telling was raised to a royal art form in the guise of jesters, court wits, or fools. In America, comedy found a home in the vaudeville circuit, the "borscht belt" in upstate New York, nightclubs, and comedy clubs.

Today, due to the collective impact of radio, network TV, cable outlets such as HBO and Comedy Central, movies, YouTube, Facebook, Snapchat, and podcasts, many cultural critics claim we are in a golden age of comedy. I agree—but more than just because of technology: comedy is everywhere because people want and need to laugh.

CHAPTER 2: HOW DO YOU MAKE FUNNY? SO, WHAT'S A JOKE?

Trying to come up with an answer to the question "What makes a joke funny?" is no easy task. Nobody has come up with a definitive algorithm to explain why a joke is funny. Various psychologists, psychiatrists, and philosophers get close, but no cigar. Joke telling and humor are too ineffable to be easily captured and codified. Like pornography, we know humor when we see it—or hear it—but we can't always figure out why it's funny.

Although nothing in joke telling is formulaic, there is an artistic calculus to comedy. There are choices to be made when concocting a comedic tale. I believe that there are four elements that determine a joke's potential acceptance or failure. When these four ingredients are in balance and harmony, the joke is a success. When one or more of these is out of whack, the result is comedic failure. These four critical ingredients are (1) *The Teller*, or the jokester; (2) *The Tale*, or the joke; (3) *The Timing*, or the right moment; and (4) *The Told*, or the audience.

CHAPTER 3: COMEDY AND COPING WITH REALITY

This chapter represents the heart and purpose of the book. Comedy and joke making are more than just foolish fun. Comedy can also serve as a safety valve or a coping mechanism for dealing with reality. Joke telling is a way of being in charge of something that we really cannot control or completely understand. Joking about a "deep topic" or a "dangerous topic" is a way of examining it in a manner that doesn't scare us, numb us, or rob us of our joy in life. Humor gives us the courage to endure that which we cannot understand or avoid. Laughter and joke telling are a way to speak the unspeakable.

CHAPTER 4: DIRTY JOKES, TASTELESS JOKES, ETHNIC JOKES

Putting aside for a moment the issue of whether a joke is ethically correct, this chapter explores the counterintuitive reasons why tasteless jokes, rude jokes, inappropriate and highly offensive jokes, and even socially harmful jokes can be considered funny. Just as the three ironclad rules of real estate are "Location, Location, Location," successful joke telling is all about "Audience, Audience, Audience." So, like it or not, nasty jokes, naughty jokes, nefarious jokes, sexual jokes, misogynistic jokes, racial jokes, or scatological jokes can, depending on the tastes and receptivity of the audience, be considered funny.

CHAPTER 5: A CONVERSATION WITH A COLLEAGUE ABOUT HUMOR AND ETHICS

Although a joke may be funny for a given audience, that does not mean that the joke is ethical. The simple fact is that some jokes are psychologically violent, abusive, dehumanizing, degrading, destructive, and damaging to particular individuals or groups. Such jokes are unethical and socially unacceptable.

This chapter will contain an interview with my colleague and friend, Ronald M. Green, former director of Dartmouth College's Ethics Institute. In our interview, Green argues that possessing a sense of humor is a critical ingredient in achieving the good life with others. He maintains that humor allows us to disassemble and deconstruct the status quo. But, he argues, jokes are not a passport to say anything. There is a "comedy code" that offers guidance about what is acceptable and unacceptable humor: Who's telling the joke? Who's hearing the joke? Who's the joke about?

Chapter 6: Philogagging: Humor in the Classroom and Beyond

I've been teaching philosophy as a required subject to classrooms full of reluctant and unwilling students for over four decades. Lately it's been harder and harder to get through to them. They seem so uninterested and unengaged. So I've been trying to seduce them into thinking philosophically by describing each course with a joke and lacing my lectures with jokes to keep them involved. I call it "enter-trainment." That is, if I can "entertain" them with a joke—if I can grab their attention and quicken their interest in what I'm saying—then maybe, just maybe, I can "train" them, or, more correctly, "educate" them, as well. But just like any stand-up comic in a club, the jokes have to be funny or I'll lose my audience.

CHAPTER 1

A Brief, Highly Selective, and Somewhat Fallacious History of Humor and Joke Telling

You know why cannibals don't eat clowns? Because they taste funny!
　—MICKEY DOLENZ (AMONG MANY, MANY, MANY OTHERS!)

Long before Mel Brooks and my Uncle Joe, humor in the form of jokes and storytelling has been part of the fabric of human experience. According to popular historian Paul Johnson, the essential concept of humor and its resultant product, laughter, can be seen as far back as 2900 BCE, when priests and scribes in ancient Egypt created a specific hieroglyph to depict the act of laughter or laughing:[1]

Johnson goes on to point out that the Middle East is also the general locale for the first recorded joke in human history. It occurred around 1500 BCE and can be found in chapter 18 of the biblical book of Genesis. Johnson claims that it is not only the first recorded joke but also the first "sex joke."

> Abraham is sitting outside his tent. Angels appear, one of whom turns out to be God. Abraham sends his wife Sarah scurrying back into the tent to prepare a meal for his guests. God gives Abraham the astounding news: "'Lo! Sarah, thy wife, shall have a son . . .' Now Abraham and Sarah were old and well stricken in age; and it ceased to be with Sarah after the manner of women. Therefore Sarah laughed within herself, saying, 'After I am waxed old shall I have pleasure, my lord, being old also?'"
>
> God was affronted by Sarah's laugh, thinking it a reflection on His powers: "Is anything too hard for the Lord?" Then Sarah denied laughing, saying, "'I laughed not,' for she was afraid." And God said, "Nay, but thou didst laugh."[2]

Johnson argues that Sarah is not laughing at God; rather, she is laughing at the idea of having intercourse with her "old man." She was laughing at the idea of Abraham getting an erection again and having sexual pleasure and then a baby, even though her menstrual cycle had ended long ago. "Ha! Sex? A baby? Ha! God, whatta guy! What a jokester!" Of course the joke is on Abraham and Sarah: they do have a baby, and they name him Isaac. And here's a fun factoid: the name "Isaac" is derived from a Hebrew word meaning *laughter*!

Historical evidence indicates that the ancient Greeks had been collecting jokes and putting them into "jokebooks" or "jestbooks" since the time of Philip II of Macedon (382–336 BCE). Like all good things that originated in Greece, the tradition of jokebooks migrated to Italy in the time of Caesar Augustus (63 BC–14 CE), and it is said that a scholar named Melissus compiled approximately 150 joke anthologies.[3] Unfortunately, only one book of humor from ancient Roman times has survived. The *Philogelos, or Laughter-Lover* is a collection of 264 jokes put together in the fourth or fifth century CE. The jokes in the collection are brief and to the point, but happily they still have a certain cachet. For example: "How shall I cut your hair?" a barber asked a customer. "In silence!" replied the wag. And: How does a man with bad breath commit suicide? He puts a bag over his head and asphyxiates himself![4]

What may be the first ethnic joke—and what is *possibly* the first Jewish joke told by a non-Jew—was allegedly told in Greece in the fifth century before the birth of Christ. Aristophanes, the Athenian playwright (446–386 BCE) is said to have written a comic play that "kills" the audience in the amphitheater with its opening joke: "Two members of the Hebrew tribe walk into a bar. They buy it! *Ta-da.*" (Just to be clear, this is an apocryphal story! It's a *joke*.)[5]

Recently, according to Latin scholar Henry Beard (*Henricus Barbatus*), historians uncovered the first recorded Latin joke, which is about Romulus and Remus (b. 771 BCE), the legendary founders of Rome.

Romulus: Quem ob rem pullus sacer viam Appiam transivit? [Translation: Why did the sacred chicken cross the Appian Way?]

Remus: Nescio. Eum evisceremus ut, extane ostensura sint illius infausti facti causam, comperimus. [Translation: I do not know. Let us cut it open and see if the entrails provide an explanation for this inauspicious behavior.][6]

And the Colosseum rocked with laughter! (And, yes, this is also apocryphal and a joke.)

In Italy, during the Renaissance, the art of the jokebook continued with the publication of Poggio Bracciolini's (1380–1459 CE) best seller *Liber Facetiarum*, or "Book of witticisms," a collection of 273 jokes, puns, and humorous anecdotes about clerical morality, obesity, flatulence, and the ever-popular priestly sexual promiscuity and drunkenness. In Shakespeare's time (1564–1616 CE), jestbooks, primarily made up of artless scatology, were all the rage.[7] And across the Atlantic during the American Civil War, Abraham Lincoln was able to find moments of diversion and laughter by reading best-selling satirists and storytellers Charles Farrar Browne, David Locke, and Robert H. Newell.[8]

In her brilliant book, *Fools Are Everywhere*, social historian Beatrice K. Otto argues that folly and foolishness are elemental characteristics of the human condition. Rascals and rogues can be found everywhere, because folly and foolishness know no boundaries. But, she argues, not all rascals are rogues, not all foolishness is folly, and we all need some rapscallion foolishness in our lives.[9]

Otto points out that, for many centuries, jesters, court wits, or fools were standard fixtures in the palaces of medieval and Renaissance Europe as well as in the corridors of power in Japan, China, India, the Middle East, and elsewhere. The job description of all these various jesters was essentially the same. Fools and jesters were licensed to tell "truth to power" without concern for censorship or reprisals. The fool's mandate was to lampoon and satirize anything and everything, even those things deemed sacrosanct. His job—for there were but a few female jesters—was to seek out and mock the absurdity of the status quo and regal expectations. The joker was the official satirist who could articulate opinions that courtiers could only silently think about.[10] A work published in 1682 on the role of fools in high places states that "jesters have a privilege which the wisest have not—they are able to do and say what the Socrates, the Scipios, and the Catos of the world dare not."[11]

The fool was granted immunity to "speak without offense." But he could never offer his commentary in earnest. He had to make use of jokes, songs, anecdotes, and improvised wit. The fool may have acted the fool, but he had to be a "sage-like fool" who used his stage persona to safely speak the truth without fear of reprisal. Every fool knew the rule: Only under the guise of foolishness can truth be tolerated. By using jokes, stories, clever badinage, the fool was held accountable for nothing.[12] From the ruler's point of view, the fool offered entertainment, the strong medicine of laughter, a release from the structured protocol of court life, perhaps an insight that could be trusted, or simply a momentary reprieve from the isolation of the office.

In England around the time of Henry VII (1457–1509 CE) the role of jesters and fools became institutionalized in the life and structure of the court. The jester's role as laugh makers and satirical pundits became a respected and much-sought-after skill set. Successful jesters became court celebrities. Their goodwill, advice, and influence were welcomed and celebrated. Some seventeenth-century English jesters served not only as fools and poets but also as tutors, private counselors, and personal emissaries sent by their masters to handle delicate diplomatic missions. Jesters of this ilk were lavishly praised, well paid, and celebrated in portraits, and they lived a life of privileged comfort.[13]

For Otto, the fool—though clad in colorful tights, caps, and bells—was neither a simple jester nor a self-indulgent clown. Rather, the fool was a confidante, a commentator, a critic, a klaxon, a siren, a town crier, a rooster in the barnyard. The fool's true calling and lasting legacy is perhaps best captured in the words of Giacomo Leopardi: "Tutto é follia in questo mondo fuorché il folleggiaré" (Everything is folly in this world except to play the fool).[14]

After reviewing the pedigree and history of jesters and fools, Otto posits that the equivalent to the court jester in modern times are stand-up comedians. Although this text argues that joke telling in all of its forms is a means and a method by which we can better understand or merely cope with the complexities of reality, I believe that the true heirs of the court jester tradition are what comic writer and film producer Paul Provenza calls *satiristas*—the satirists. For Provenza, satirists are not just comedians or jokesters. They are comics with an edge. They are contrarians or comedic critics who intentionally set out to belittle, debunk, and/or deconstruct the political and social status quo.[15] Like poets Alexander Pope and Horace, Provenza believes that satire should wound and harm.[16]

It is, of course, difficult to deny the talent and humorous effect of such comedic legends as Bob Hope (1903–2003), Milton Berle (1908–2002), George Burns (1896–1996), or Joan Rivers (1933–2014). (I am, by the way, referring to the early incarnation of Joan Rivers, who only told mildly naughty jokes, and long before she specialized in explicit, salacious humor and celebrity sexual put-downs.) But these comedians were primarily joke tellers who came out of the tradition of vaudeville, the borscht circuit, and nightclubs. Their objective was to entertain, to titillate, to get a laugh, but not to intentionally or regularly be socially or politically profound or prophetic. They thought of themselves as being in "show business." They told jokes intended to please, to produce a smile. They were trying to earn a living and were not out to change the world. They may have used satire in their jokes, but they were not satirists. Here's a little sample of their work.

I said to my wife, "Do you feel the excitement has gone out of our marriage?" She said, "I'll discuss it with you during the next commercial break."

—Milton Berle

I love flying. Why, I've been to almost as many places as my luggage.

—Bob Hope

All my mother ever told me about sex was that a man goes on top and the women on the bottom. So, for three years my husband and I slept in a bunk bed!

—Joan Rivers

I personally stay away from natural foods. At my age I need all the preservatives that I can get.

—George Burns

A question, given the ages of these comics, and the fact that they kept performing well into their eighties and nineties: Isn't there another book waiting to be written on comedy and longevity??

Satire, at its core, is different from just telling innocuous jokes and clever stories. Satire, the sarcastic comment ("sarcasm" is from the Greek word *sarkazein*—"to rend the flesh, to chew the lips in rage"), is the use of taunting, sneering, or cutting remarks in an attempt to annoy, expose, make sense of, denounce, or deride a perceived folly or vice. Although a primary purpose of satire is to be humorous or produce a laugh, satire isn't always presented in the form of a perfectly structured joke. More often than not, it's presented as a zinger, a choreographed comment, a one-liner, or a humorous bullet-point observation. But what satire shares with joke telling is that there is always a punch line, a specific message, a particular point of view.

Academy award–winning actor and comic Robin Williams (1951–2014) argued that the job of satire is to "point out that even the pope farts. To give us a common humanity, to say these are our weaknesses; they come along with our strengths." To deny our weakness, said Williams, is to lose track of our humanity, to lose track of who we really are.[17]

Todd Hanson—longtime contributor to the wildly successful satirical newspaper the *Onion* (now, ironically, exclusively available online)—mirrors Williams's comments. Hanson argues that the human condition is inherently flawed and deserving of ridicule. Nothing should be safe. Nothing is inappropriate. There is nothing that we shouldn't make light of. Denial and diversion, Hanson suggests, isn't sufficient. It's not enough to just entertain people. Satirists use comedy to point out things that make them angry. Satire allows us to vent our rage by making as much fun as possible of those things that drive us mad. The job of the satirists is to confront the uncomfortable, the unanswerable, the unspeakable. The job of satire, says Hanson, is "to vex the world."[18]

Some stand-up comics just tell jokes, take clever potshots at life, ridicule it, tease it, laugh at it. Satirists attack it, deconstruct it, mock it. But both groups seem to agree with legendary comic Groucho Marx about comedians: "If it weren't for the brief respite we give the world with our foolishness, the world would see a mass suicide in numbers that compare favorably with the death rate of lemmings."[19] Like Groucho, I'm convinced that the true subtext of all forms of humor is to help us navigate, mitigate, and tolerate the complexities and mysteriousness of life. Without laughter, without comedy, life would be too difficult to endure.

Many commentators on popular culture have suggested that we are in the midst of a golden age of comedy. More specifically, many contend that we are in a golden age of stand-up comedy. Although there is a long history of comedy venues and clubs— the Ice House (Pasadena), the Punchline (Atlanta), Comedy Underground (Seattle), Dangerfield's (New York), Laugh Factory (Los Angeles), the Purple Onion (San Francisco)—the last twenty years have witnessed, across the entertainment landscape, an explosion of small private clubs and franchise clubs, such as Zanies, the Improv, and Uncle Vinnie's. These establishments are not copycat Second Cities or traditional night-clubs. They are clubs exclusively devoted to stand-up comedy. There's no band or dancing between acts. There are no musical interludes. It's usually just two comics—a headliner and a warm-up act—doing two to three sets a night. There's a cover charge, a two-drink minimum, and a not-so-funny reminder to "be sure to tip your server!"

Until recently, most comics did their work in small, compact rooms with a capacity of between one hundred and two hundred seats. A "big gig" was to get booked at theaters and auditoriums holding twelve hundred to four thousand seats. Today, according to the *Wall Street Journal*, there are between a hundred and two hundred "comic superstars" who can fill such jumbo spaces as New York's Madison Square Garden, as has Jim Gaffigan, or the Nassau Coliseum, home of the NHL's New York Islanders, which hosted Amy Schumer, or Philadelphia's Lincoln Financial Field, which headlined Kevin Hart. In the summer of 2015, Hart filled Lincoln Financial Field with over fifty-three thousand screaming fans. It is reported that in 2013 Hart's Let Me Explain tour—and movie of the same title—grossed $32.3 million. And in 2008 German comic Mario Birth established a world record for live comedy, performing for seventy thousand people in Berlin's Olympic Stadium.[20]

In a very real sense, this golden age of comedy started with the eight hundred–pound gorilla of comedy, *Saturday Night Live*. For forty-plus years, SNL has introduced and showcased some of the best comic minds and performers in the business. Although the show is primarily based on skits and quick blackout gags—not stand-up routines—SNL has set the table and helped to create a general appetite for comedy in all forms.

Another major factor that propels this new golden age of comedy can be attributed to cable television and the success of the comedy special format. The formula for these specials is very straightforward and easy to do: A fairly well-known or a hot comic talent, a large auditorium filled to the brim with paying customers (thereby defraying some of the costs of production), a basic three-camera shoot, good lighting, and great sound, and, bingo, you are in show business. Netflix, HBO, Showtime, Comedy Central, and Epix are all players in the field. On occasion, even staid and steady PBS gets a piece of the action. Besides television, of course, there's been a comedic explosion on the airwaves as well. Satellite radio has a number of channels dedicated to comedy. Even socially serious NPR has a comedy show that's a runaway national hit—*Wait Wait . . . Don't Tell Me*, with Peter Sagal.

Perhaps cable TV's greatest contributions to the comedic landscape are live shows that have changed the social impact of comedy and importance of political satire and news analysis. I'm referring, of course, to *The Daily Show* (Craig Kilborn/Jon Stewart/Trevor Noah), *The Colbert Report* (Steven Colbert), *The Nightly Show* (Larry Wilmore), *Last Week Tonight* (John Oliver), *Real Time with Bill Maher*, and, most recently, *Full Frontal* (Samantha Bee). The respective hosts of these shows essentially play the part of comic–political reporter–pundit.

Their task is to mock and chastise almost everything and everyone in the news and society at large. No one, not Democrats, Republicans, liberals, conservatives, Libertarians, vegetarians, Tea Partiers, teetotalers, polygamists, xenophobes, nuns, or autoerotic-asphyxiation devotees, is above or beyond the reach of their commentary and criticism.

Finally, the age of the Internet also has contributed both quantitatively and qualitatively to our collective interest in and appetite for comedy. At the level of sheer quantity, simply direct your favorite search engine to "lists of jokes" and be prepared to be overwhelmed with joke options that range from "Jokes for Kids" to "Jokes So Stupid They're Actually Funny" to "Jokes So Filthy You'll Need to Take a Shower." But, more important, beyond the ability to store and reproduce an endless list of jokes, the greatest gift that the Internet affords comedy lovers everywhere is access to Facebook, Twitter, Instagram, YouTube, Vine, and Periscope. Professional comedians, would-be comedians, and amateurs alike are now able to post jokes, skits, stand-up routines, comedic playlets, and Web series to a vast potential audience waiting for them in virtual reality. Of course, the best example of the nexus between the Internet and comedy is podcasts. Podcasts allow comedy lovers to subscribe to a particular comic's series or to cherry-pick other episodes on iTunes for frequently produced comedic content. Podcasts have educated a new generation of "comedy nerds" by exposing them to new comedians and to long interviews of comedians by fellow comedians about the nature of comedy. Got a favorite comic?

Look them up on YouTube. Chances are, if they have been filmed, videotaped, or audio recorded, you'll find them there. Want to be a comic? All you need is a user ID and a password, and you, too, can potentially be a comedy star!

And yet, even as this comedy avalanche began its thunderous roll, the *New York Times* declared that "The Joke Is Dead." No one tells jokes anymore, declared the *Times*. To tell a joke is to dub yourself a "cornball." Jokes are a "high social crime." Jokes are "politically incorrect." Jokes have simply "gone out of fashion." They are the "kiss of death."[21]

If the editors at the *New York Times* meant that very few, if any, comics make a career out of walking out on stage and reciting a long list of disconnected jokes, starting with "A man walks in to a bar . . ." building to "A priest, a rabbi, and a minister . . ." and concluding with "Did you hear about the talking parrot?" then I agree—nobody does that anymore. Today's professional comedians rarely rattle off one-liners or deliver a long series of disconnected jokes. Today's comedians are raconteurs and social observers. They tell a story, stick with a theme, and offer quirky observations about the topic they are examining as they go along. Comedian and best-selling author Aziz Ansari argues that, in a strange way, comedy is a lot like sociology: Comedy is about observing the culture around you, observing what people do, and then making jokes about what they observe. Comedians are observers and commentators as much as they are joke tellers.[22]

When I was growing up, the "star of stars" of this tradition was Myron Cohen (1902–1986). This elegant, well-dressed man would walk on stage and simply tell a series of stories and jokes, more often than not in a Jewish or Italian accent, about common events in ethnic neighborhoods and of immigrant domestic life. Long before he became persona non grata, Bill Cosby pretty much did the same thing—only, of course, as a black man and without a Jewish or Italian accent. Cosby told stories and jokes about his father's parenting style and his own style of parenting. He told stories, with jokes inside of them, about "Fat Albert" and the group of guys he grew up with. He told stories and jokes about his wife. He told stories and jokes about going to college and his brief flirtation with the NFL.

The megastar of contemporary storytellers or "observational comedians" is, arguably, Jerry Seinfeld. Whether starring in his hugely popular TV series, *Seinfeld* (1989–1998), or on stage, what he really does for a living is storytelling. In essence, Seinfeld unpacks, examines, and ridicules the obvious, the banal, the commonsensical stuff in our lives that we rarely take time to scrutinize closely. It's as if he's having a conversation with the audience. He stands up in front of a crowd and opens with lines like "Have you ever thought about the difference between men and women and how they write a check?" Or he discusses the protocol of regifting an unwanted present. Or he carefully unpacks the sexual etiquette of the fourth date. Or he tells us "why smoking is certainly one of the oddest and stupidest of human idiosyncrasies." In effect, he is telling us jokes wrapped up in stories about the "stuff" in our lives. Even in his new Web series, *Comedians in Cars Getting Coffee*, the title says it all. There is no script for the show: Jerry picks up a fellow comic in an antique or unusual car, and they drive to a diner, order coffee, and tell each other funny stories and jokes about things that happen to them working as comics and about life in general.

Of course, the heir apparent to Seinfeld's throne is his former opening act and mentee, Louis C.K. Although C.K. has written for other comics, and writes, directs, edits, and produces his five-time Emmy Award–wining TV show, *Louie*, "stand-up is, was, and ever shall be his first love and his true calling."[23] Louis C.K. gets up on stage, presenting himself "as a bumbling everyman," and reflects on the "minutia of day-to-day life."[24] In his eighty-minute set he shares his comedic reflections on marriage, divorce, raising children, getting stoned, going to the IMAX, why he hates cell phones, loneliness, selfishness, why he likes being rich versus being poor, and why being "white" is so cool! As one commentator succinctly put it, Louis C.K. "knows how to deliver universal truths wrapped in sometimes uncomfortable laughs. For example, 'Running away will not solve your problems,' he said . . . discussing suicide, 'But killing yourself will.'"[25]

No matter the headlines in the *New York Times*, joke telling is alive and well. I agree with Garrison Keillor, of *Prairie Home Companion* fame, that what's dead are practical jokes, whoopee-cushion jokes, removing all four tires from our bachelor uncle's car on a Saturday night. But the telling of jokes, says Keillor, remains a necessary and stable feature of amiable conversation and a requirement of civilized society. No matter how educated you are, says Keillor, you may never need to use your knowledge of math or physics, but the ability to tell a good joke often comes in handy. Bottom line, according to Keillor walking around with the *New York Times* doesn't necessarily prove that you are smart, but if you can tell a joke, that, for sure, means you're okay! Being able to tell a joke, onstage or anywhere, helps you feel better about yourself, helps make people like you, and puts others at their ease. Joke telling, concludes Keillor, is both a thrill and a gift.[26]

CHAPTER 2

How Do You Make Funny?
So, What's a Joke?

Analyzing humor is like dissecting a frog. Few people are interested, and the frog dies of it.

—E. B. WHITE

Folklorist Alan Dundes has argued (his tongue firmly affixed to the inside of his cheek) that there are two classic theories regarding the origin of contemporary jokes and joke telling. One theory is that jokes come from stockbrokers and financial analysts, who have both time on their hands between sales and a well-established communication network to send jokes to friends, family, and customers. The second theory maintains that jokes come out of the penal system, where prisoners have a lot of time on their hands as well as a captive audience. Of course, says Dundes, modern scholarship indicates that lately these two theories have merged into one.[1] (Badda bing, badda boom! Thank you, ladies and gentleman, and please tell your friends that we're doing two shows a night!)

Of course, the origin of joke telling isn't as simple as that, and, as I've already indicated, jokes and joke telling stretch back to ancient Egypt, Greece, and Rome. The purpose of this chapter is more hands-on than historical. I want to examine the art of creating and telling jokes. Please allow me to apologize in advance, because, in order to do this, we need to start by examining, ever so briefly, three classic theories that philosophers (Lord, save us!) have come up with to explain why we find humor in and laugh at jokes: the Superiority Theory, the Incongruity Theory, and the Relief Theory.

SUPERIORITY THEORY

Essentially, this theory claims that we laugh at other people's failings, inabilities, and inadequacies. At one end of the spectrum, the Superiority Theory communicates ridicule, contempt, derision, aggression, and scorn for others not like us. At the other end of the spectrum, the theory results in farce and satire. The Superiority Theory is about "one-upmanship," or "let them eat cake," "wounding," "distancing," or a "put-down attitude" toward others.

Two strangers meet.

TEXAN: Hi, where are you from?

HARVARD GRADUATE: I come from a place where we do not end sentences with prepositions!

TEXAN: Okay—where are you from, Asshole?[2]

Incongruity Theory

This theory maintains that amusement is about the unexpected, the mismatched, the illogical, and the misalignment of ideas, circumstances, or events in our lives. The point here is a simple one: We live in an orderly world. We have expectations about the structure of reality and the patterns of language. So, when patterns, properties, or events are altered, we are amused.

> Did you see me at Princess Diana's funeral? I was the one who started the Mexican wave!

> A professor of logic is on a plane when the captain announces that they've lost one of their four engines, so they'll be delayed one hour in landing.
>
> About an hour later the captain announces that a second engine is out and that there will be a three-hour delay in landing.
>
> Again, an hour later the captain reports that they've lost the third engine and that there will be a seven-hour delay in landing.
>
> At which point the professor turns to his seatmate and says, "My heavens, if we lose one more engine, we'll be up here all day!"

Relief Theory

The best-known version of this theory is developed by the father of psychoanalysis, Sigmund Freud. He thought that laughter provides pleasure because it economizes on the energy that would ordinarily be used to contain or repress a disturbing emotional activity. In other words, "a joke transforms a serious conflict into a trivial one and thereby releases emotional tension."[3] Freud's example of the theory is less clear, or perhaps just less funny, than it ought to be: "As a criminal is being led out to the courtyard to be hung on a Monday morning, he observes, 'Well, this is a good beginning to the week!'"[4] Freud suggests that the prisoner's gallows humor momentarily frees us from our natural fear of death and allows us to jest about the very thing we fear.[5]

Unfortunately, the only thing that these theories prove is that theories on humor are definitely not humorous. These three theories are simply not rich enough or nuanced enough to capture and explain the compound complexity of a comedic moment or why we laugh at jokes. As Bob Mankoff, long-time cartoon editor at the New Yorker, succinctly points out, "Although humor is a fascinating topic, academics being academics can take the fun out of it and make it boring."[6]

While statistically speaking it's probably true that Cicero was correct when he suggested that "the most common kind of joke is that in which we expect one thing and another is said,"[7] there is nevertheless no one formula, no one theory, no single algorithm, that can explain, define, and predict humor, laughter, or successful joke telling. To paraphrase the words of G. K. Chesterton, humor, like religion, is a mystery and can never be simply rationalized.

Ted Cohen, the man who "literally" wrote the book on jokes (*Jokes: Philosophical Thoughts on Joking Matters*), has concluded that "there is no formula for making jokes, and not everyone can do it." Just as there are no exact recipes for creating figures of speech and works of art, there are none for jokes. However, although there is no science behind it, for Cohen there is a method, a logic, to humor and joke telling. But, he insists, there are no guarantees that anyone will think that the "joke was funny."[8]

In 2001, British psychologist Richard Wiseman indirectly proved Cohen's contention that there is no one fixed formula to determine if and why a joke is funny. Wiseman and his colleagues set out to find the world's funniest joke. He was in search of a joke that had universal appeal and acceptance. They set up a website, LaughLab, where people were encouraged to submit jokes as well as rate jokes from other contributors. More than forty thousand jokes were submitted, and nearly two million people from forty different countries voted on the "giggle factor" of the submissions. In October 2002, Wiseman proclaimed that he and his team had come up with the world's funniest joke. And, ta-da, here it is:

Two hunters are out in the woods when one of them collapses. He doesn't seem to be breathing, and his eyes are glazed. The other guy whips out his phone and calls emergency services. He gasps, "My friend is dead! What can I do?" The operator says, "Calm down.

I can help. First, let's make sure he's dead." There is a silence, then a gunshot. Back on the phone, the guy says, "Okay, now what?"[9]

Question: Is this joke really that funny? And, if it really isn't all that funny, why does it deserve the title of World's Funniest Joke?

In retrospect, not even Wiseman thinks it's that funny. "It's terrible," said Wiseman. "I think [what] we found is the world's cleanest, blandest, and most internationally accepted joke." In fact, what the "giggleometer" came up with is a joke that the least number of people find offensive! At best, it's ho-hum. It's sort of funny, and it doesn't offend anyone. As Wiseman sadly concludes, "It's the color beige in joke form."[10] So much for the "wise" in Wiseman.

Talent advisor and comic coach Dave Schwensen argues that there are only two rules of comedy: Rule 1: There are no rules. Rule 2: See Rule 1.[11] I agree, and yet, although comedy and joke telling is not formulaic, there is an artistic calculus to comedy. There are choices we make in concocting a comedic tale. Although jokes come in every topic, shape, and size, there are a few principles that underlie a joke's potential acceptance and success.

Jokes are laughable, funny, enjoyable—or not—depending upon four basic elements:

Four Elements of Joke Telling

The Teller	The Joker
The Tale	The Joke
The Timing	The Right Moment
The Told	The Audience

THE TELLER

The comic, the entertainer, or the ordinary person telling the joke needs a certain amount of verbal and theatrical skill to be a successful joker. Delivery is critical. Does the teller have a decent "stage" presence? Are they clear, confident? Do they project well? Are they charming, intriguing, unusual? Are they good mimics? Do they do dialects well? The bottom line for all jokes, whether on stage or at a dinner party, is that successful presentations require a certain amount of acting, rhythm, and good pacing. Telling a joke "involves a careful control of pauses, hesitations, silences, and knowing exactly when to deliver the punch line; like selling the lyrics of a song, jokes need to be expressed in an engaging manner."[12]

THE TALE

The joke itself has to be interesting or clever, or unusual or unexpected, or profound or profane, or something that arrests, shocks, surprises, delights, or disgusts the intended audience. According to writer, director, actor, and comic Mel Brooks, "comedy must be daring. It must skirt the edge of bad taste. If it doesn't, it's not challenging or exciting—or funny."[13]

Although there are no guarantees that a joke will be funny and that the audience will laugh, a certain amount of experience, discernment, discretion, and eye for quality control separates the successful from the unsuccessful jokester. For example, it seems to me that no experienced comic or joke teller over the age of seven would try to win friends and influence people by using such non-knee-slapping ditties as

Q: What did the grape say when the rhinoceros trampled it?

A: Not much. It just let out a little wine!

or

Q: What did the big chimney say to the little chimney?

A: Nothing! Chimneys can't talk.

THE TIMING

Timing is much more than pacing the delivery of the joke. Timing, in a larger sense, is about the appropriateness of the joke in the moment. Timing and circumstance can never be overlooked. Every comic and joke teller needs to determine when it is appropriate to tell a particular joke. When is the joke too soon? When is the subject matter too close for comfort? When is it too distant to matter? Where's the sweet spot? When is it too raw, too horrifying, too as-yet-undigested to make fun of?

In March 2011, an earthquake and tsunami hit Japan, causing widespread property damage and, in the end, claiming an estimated ten thousand lives. Soon after the event, comedian Gilbert Gottfried posted ten jokes to his personal Twitter feed about the catastrophe. (This is the same Gilbert Gottfried who had received severe criticism regarding a joke he made "too soon" post-9/11 about an "airplane that made an unscheduled stop at the Empire State Building.") A few examples are more than enough to give you a flavor of Gilbert's attempt to find humor "too soon" after this tragic Japanese tsunami:

"I just split up with my girlfriend, but like the Japanese say, 'They'll be another one floating by any minute now.'"

"I was talking to my Japanese real estate agent. I said 'is there a school in this area.' She said 'not now, but just wait.'"

"Japan called me. They said: 'Maybe those jokes are a hit in the US, but over here, they're all sinking.'"

"Japan is really advanced. They don't go to the beach. The beach comes to them."

Gottfried argued that it was all in jest. Some of his die-hard fans agreed, but his employer, Aflac Inc.—for whom 75 percent of revenue is derived from the Japanese market and with whom Gottfried had a long-term, multimillion-dollar TV commercial contract—fired him for making comments "lacking in humor and good taste."[14]

George Bernard Shaw, Groucho Marx, and a host of others have suggested that "humor is tragedy plus time." But would any amount of time be enough to make the tragedy of 9/11 or Japan's tsunami funny or objects of humor? Maybe, maybe not. It can, of course, be argued that with enough time almost anything is possible. Almost nothing is sacred. Almost nothing is above satirical ridicule. For example, Mel Brooks certainly made a joke and a fortune out of Hitler and Nazi Germany in his movie (1968) and play (2001) *The Producers*. And the Monty Python gang made outrageous fun of all of Christianity in their satirical take on Jesus Christ's life and crucifixion in *The Life of Brian* (1979). Perhaps Mark Twain found the "timing sweet spot" when he suggested that one should never enter a funeral laughing and telling jokes, but one should never leave a funeral without telling a joke and sharing a laugh about the deceased.[15] Depending on when and how you tell them, jokes can be a bomb or a balm, a stab or a salve.

THE TOLD

The ultimate target and judge of both successful and unsuccessful jokes is, of course, the audience. Without an audience, joke telling is a purely theoretical exercise. The joker and the audience are in a symbiotic relationship. For jokes to work, both must share the same geography of life. Both must partake in, or be aware of, the same cultural traits and markers. And, of course, because lifestyles, languages, and cultures are so diverse, there is no such thing as a pure joke, a universal joke, or a joke that would make sense and be funny to everyone.

Ted Cohen argues that all jokes are conditional—that is, all jokes have conditional requirements connecting the teller and the audience, or common knowledge, common background, common language, common cultural presuppositions, prejudices, and myths. When a joke works, it's because the joker is telling a story and using assumptions, knowledge, cultural references, and a background that an audience recognizes, understands, and can react and respond to. The most elemental reason why jokes do not work is because we do not all share the same life experiences, the same frames of reference. In the end, we are a society divided by different tastes because we are a society of different backgrounds and experiences.[16] The conditional nature of joke telling explains why jokes, comics, and comedy are so subjective, community-specific, generational, or niche-based. Joke telling is like popular music: Popular or commercial music primarily speaks to a very specific audience, a very specific demographic slice of the total pie. That is why most parents and children are surprised and amazed by what each of them considers listenable, enjoyable, danceable popular songs and singers. I remember my father saying to me, "Elvis screams, Sinatra sings!"

My favorite undergraduate philosophy professor once said that the main problem with existentialism, as a movement, is that there are as many definitions of existentialism as there are existentialists. The same thing can be said of trying to come up with a systematic typology of jokes. The simple fact is that there are as many kinds of jokes as there are joke tellers. Jokes can be found on every topic—from the mundane to the ridiculous to the sublime. Jokes can be juvenile or highly esoteric, common-sensical, sexual, urbane or sophomoric, Homeric or pedestrian.

However, according to stand-up comic Lewis Black, all jokes, long or short, and on any and all topics, tell a story, paint a picture, and offer off-centered, skewed, absurd, ridic-ulous, and/or ribald reflections on the complicated, confusing thing we call life. And the structure of all jokes, says Lewis, is elegantly simple: First, there's the set-up statement or the story line. Second, there is the pause or a brief punctuation. Finally, there is a punch line, a conclusion, a resolution, or an answer. And, he suggests, when you push jokes and joke telling back to fundamentals, there are really only five kinds of jokes: the long shaggy dog story, the shorter narrative joke, the formulaic joke, the quickie, and the one-liner. Here are a few examples of each.[17]

Shaggy Dog Joke

Supposedly once literally about shaggy dogs, but no one knows for sure. The basic structure of this type of joke is a long narration of unimportant or redundant facts and incidents that ultimately results in an absurd, irrelevant, or totally unexpected punch line. Nowadays the shaggy dog joke is simply a synonym for a long-form joke.

A couple in their seventies are both having problems remembering things. During a checkup, the doctor tells them that they're physically okay, but they might want to start writing things down to help them remember.

Later that night, while watching TV, the old man gets up from his chair. "Want anything while I'm in the kitchen?" he asks.

"Will you get me a bowl of ice cream?"

"Sure."

"Don't you think you should write it down so you can remember it?" she asks.

"No, I can remember it."

"Well, I'd like some strawberries on top, too. Maybe you should write it down, so as not to forget it?"

He says, "I can remember that. You want a bowl of ice cream with strawberries."

"I'd also like whipped cream. I'm certain you'll forget that; write it down," she says.

Irritated, he says, "I don't need to write it down; I can remember it! Ice cream with strawberries and whipped cream—I got it, for goodness sake!"

Then he toddles into the kitchen. After about twenty minutes, the old man returns from the kitchen and hands his wife a plate of bacon and eggs. She stares at the plate for a moment and then says, "So, where's my toast?"

NARRATIVE JOKE

A Jewish guy goes into a confessional and says, "Hello, Father, my name is Gary Stein, and I'm currently involved with a thirty-five-year-old woman and her beautiful twenty-nine-year-old sister. Each night for hours and hours we engage in all manner of sexual pleasure, and in my entire life I've never felt better or happier."

"My good man," says the priest, "I think you've come to the wrong place. Why are you telling me this?"

And the guy says, "Because I'm seventy-nine years old and I'm telling everybody!"

A SHORT, SHORT NARRATIVE JOKE

Catholic girls make the best lesbians. Their whole life they've been told, "Don't have sex with men. It's a sin!" They're like "Oh, okay, I can do that!"

—Judy Carter

FORMULAIC JOKES
Knock-Knocks

Knock, knock.

Who's there?

Absent minded.

Absent minded who?

I'm sorry, what?

Knock, knock.

Who's there?

Repeat.

Repeat who?

Okay. Who, who, who, who . . .

Elephant Jokes

Q: How do you stop an elephant from charging?

A: Take away his credit card.

Q: How do you get an elephant out of the theater?

A: You can't! It's in their blood.

Light Bulb Jokes

Q: How many conservative economists does it take to change a light bulb?

A: None! The darkness will cause the light bulb to change by itself.

Q: How many bureaucrats does it take to screw in a light bulb?

A: Two—one to assure everyone that everything possible is being done, while the other screws the bulb into the water faucet.

Lawyer Jokes

The Devil meets a young lawyer and says to him, "Listen, give me your soul and the souls of your wife and children, and I'll make you a senior managing partner of your firm." The lawyer stares at him for a moment and says, "So, what's the catch?"

You find yourself trapped in a room with a murderer, a rapist, and a lawyer. You have a revolver with only two bullets. What do you do?

Shoot the lawyer! Twice!

QUICKIES

Secret to a happy marriage? Simple! Dinner and dancing twice a week. I go on Tuesdays, she goes on Thursdays.

—Henny Youngman

A hooker told me she'd do anything for $300. So, I gave her the money and told her to paint my house!

—Henny Youngman

I don't get no respect. As a kid, I'd play hide-and-seek and the other kids wouldn't even look for me.

—Rodney Dangerfield

When I was a kid, I got no respect. I told my mother, "I'm gonna run away from home." She said, "On your mark . . ."

—Rodney Dangerfield

ONE-LINERS

I never forget a face, but I'll make an exception in your case.

—Groucho Marx

Marriage is a great institution, but I'm not ready for an institution yet.

—Mae West

Although many of these jokes are tried and true, and although some have been delivered to audiences by "comedic stars," there is no way to predict whether a fresh audience will find these jokes funny or even mildly amusing. Unfortunately, even when a joke *teller* does his/her due diligence regarding the *tale*, the *timing*, and those to whom it's *told*, audiences can find a joke benign, boring, tedious, unsophisticated, offensive, or utterly uninteresting. Comedy savant Andrew Hudgins argues that, good intentions and preparation aside, "jokes either work, or they don't. You are either a funny man or a fool."[18] When a joke "flops"—fails—the teller and the told did not connect; for whatever reason, the target audience failed to respond.

Ted Cohen wishes there were a way to diagnose and correct this state of affairs, but there isn't. People respond eccentrically to humor. When I laugh at a joke and you don't, what can be concluded? Nothing, really—only that sometimes we have similar responses, but sometimes we are different, and that sometimes we can explain this difference and sometimes we can't.[19] Every student of comedy, every working comic, wishes there were an answer, a tried-and-true formula to correct this problem. But, regrettably, there isn't.

Virtually every professional comic has bombed on stage. The lights go up, you're introduced, you're in front of the mic, and you're giving them your best stuff, material that has worked before, and yet . . . nothing! Literally, nothing! No applause! No laughs! No boos! No heckling! Not even a little nervous coughing. The only sound disrupting the silence is the tinkling of ice in a glass as the audience tries to use alcohol to blunt the awkwardness of a clumsy moment.

It's moments like these that make every comedian realize the full impact of Steve Martin's lament that "doing comedy alone on stage is the ego's last stand."[20] Depending on how the show goes, it's either elation or misery. And when you flop, all that's left for the aspiring comedian is to quit the stage and give up show business or to recommit. And what recommitment comes down to is the Comedic Rule of Five Ps: Practice, practice, practice, practice, and practice!

CHAPTER 3

Comedy and Coping with Reality

I call laughter a safety valve. When you are depressed . . . you don't say, "Let's go see Virginia Woolf," you say, "Let's go laugh."

—JERRY LEWIS

If I'm laughing, you know I'm either very happy or very sad. . . . I cope with things with jokes.

—CRISTELA ALONZO

After studying comedy for more years than I care to admit, I've only been able to come up with a few firm convictions on the topic. For one, humor, from pie-in-the-face slapstick to sophisticated cerebral satire, seems to be a universal feature of the human condition. Two, there is no Platonic ideal of the perfect joke or the perfect joke formula. Three, different folks like different jokes. Four, when you have to diagram a joke, explain how it works, and why it's funny, then the joke ceases to be funny. Five, notwithstanding the truth of the above four propositions, there is a certain purity, grace, satisfaction, and artistry in a well-structured, well-told, well-received joke. As many scholars of language have pointed out, there is something remarkable, wonderful, and perhaps even magical about the special power, gift, or talent that we have as a species to delight others, as well as ourselves, with words and little fictitious narratives that we call jokes.[1]

I am also convinced that there are at least three goals or benefits to be derived from the act and art of joke telling and the pursuit of humor: pleasure and delight, the development of relationships, and a defense mechanism.

PLEASURE AND DELIGHT

No matter what else can be said about comedy, and no matter how sophisticated a theory one can concoct to explain humor, the bottom line remains elemental: as a rule, most of us find pleasure in joke telling. Some jokes are simply meant to be silly, to titillate. Others are meant to be outrageous, shocking, ridiculous, or subversive. Some are smart, intelligent, or profound. Still others try to be profane, prurient, or pornographic. Some jokes are highly metaphysical, while others are deeply metaphorical. And yet the attempt of all jokes and joke tellers is to, at least momentarily, arrest the attention of the listeners and offer them a novel, distorted, unusual, comedically skewed take on reality that will result in pleasure, delight, surprise, and/or laughter.

Even when a joke fails, I am convinced that no joke teller intentionally sets out to tell a joke that they didn't think was funny. Even a groaner—a joke that elicits a groan or moan but not a guffaw—is meant to be humorous. For example, here's my favorite, almost-naughty, groaner joke.

Q: What do you do with an elephant with three balls?

A: Walk him and pitch to the rhino.

Now, if you are a baseball fan, you may find yourself grinning, groaning, smiling, and/or smirking at this piece of sophomoric wordplay, but I doubt that it will elicit convulsive laughter. And even if you're not a baseball fan, the absurdity of the concept and the wordplay make it kind of funny—that is, a groaner.

The pleasure and delight that can be elicited by joke telling is a two-way street. The delight is shared by both the teller and the told. Most people find pleasure in hearing jokes, and many—but not all—people enjoy telling jokes. Jokers are trying to be playful and offer pleasure with their witticisms. Like the thoughtful and conscientious lover, they want to pleasure their partner or audience, and in so doing they themselves achieve pleasure. In other words, the teller/lover enjoys the act itself, as well as the satisfaction it produces in the told/ partner.

Robin Williams was a troubled comic genius who openly admitted that much of his own humor and energy was driven by a personal sense of pain. Nonetheless, he loved to perform. And even more than movies and TV sitcoms, he loved to do stand-up. The immediacy of stand-up, the give-and-take, the delivery and the feedback, helped him put aside his own pain while at the same time giving pleasure to others. It gave him, he said, a "combination of serenity and exhilaration."[2]

Local Chicago comic and longtime friend Aaron Freeman doesn't look at being a stand-up comedian as therapy or escapism, but, rather, as the greatest job he could ever have. "Think about it," he once said. "I'm around really smart, creative types [writers and other comics] all the time. We talk politics, comedy—you name it. But what this gig is really about is getting up all alone in front of a group of people and making them laugh. Making their sides ache. Making their eyes water. Making them get lost in the moment. . . . All of a sudden," Aaron continued, "I've got a room full of people who like me, who laugh with me, who applaud me! And I'm up there really having fun too! Man, it's a rush. Drugs are good, but, believe me, this is better! Much better! It's even better than sex . . . No! Wait! Not really! But it comes close at times! You know, most people hate their jobs. Not me! My job is to make people happy. How cool is that? And they pay me for it too!"[3]

Years after this conversation I came across a quotation from writer and comic Carl Reiner that both reinforces and adds another dimension to Aaron's comedic point of view: "Inviting people to laugh with you while you are laughing at yourself is a good thing to do. You may be the fool, but you're the fool in charge."[4]

RELATIONSHIPS

American poet Andrew Hudgins claims in his totally honest, often hilarious, and too-often-painful memoir, *The Joker*, that he has used humor and joke telling for his entire life as a way of making others recognize him, react to him, and like him. Growing up in a near "humorless household," Hudgins nevertheless regularly bombarded his parents with jokes. Their usual response was "Quit making a show of yourself." They never thought of him as particularly funny, but at least he got their attention for a while.

Because his father was in the US Air Force, the family moved frequently; consequently, he was always the new kid in school. Jokes were a way for Hudgins to be cool and accepted, or at least tolerated, by his ever-changing stream of classmates. In college and graduate school, he figured out that being a jokester, flashing a bit of wit, was considered a sign of intelligence with his male classmates and a turn-on with the ladies. As a young professor, he discovered that well-modulated humor was his passport to social and professional acceptance. Humor freed him from his sense of isolation. Joke telling, even when he exceeded the boundaries of good taste and respectability, afforded him attention, recognition, and relationships.[5]

Humor *is* a way to reach out to people. Jokes can be used as a mitzvah—a blessed favor—a gift we can give to one another. Successful jokes are a means we use to establish rapport and possible intimacy with others. Jokes are an enticement. They lure people in. In the laughter that ensues from a well-told joke, we are able to overcome animosity and pre-established social and cultural barriers. To paraphrase Ted Cohen, when I tell a joke, I want to reach you. I want to verify that we understand each other. I want to see if we are, at least, a little alike. I want to establish a relationship.[6]

As Victor Borge suggested, jokes are "the shortest distance between two people."[7] Jokes are an olive branch we extend to one another. Jokes attempt to be kind, to be convivial. Jokes are an attempt to mitigate hostility, reduce tension, demonstrate our shared humanity, and remind us of our commonality. Jokes can be an attempt to reach out and commiserate with others. Jokes are also an attempt to change the mood and the tone of an otherwise awkward or unpleasant situation.

Perhaps the best example I've ever encountered regarding the ability of humor to smooth ruffled feathers and help put things in perspective is a very long shaggy dog joke in the form of a letter written by a college student to her parents.

Dear Mom and Dad,

I'm sorry for not writing sooner but hope you'll understand. First, sit down before you read further.

I'm doing much better now after recovering from the concussion I received from jumping out of my dorm window in the fire last month. I can almost see normally thanks to the loving care of Norman, the janitor who pulled me from the flames. He more than saved me; he's become my whole life. I have been living with him since the fire, and we are planning to get married before my pregnancy shows.

Yes, I'm pregnant. I knew you'd be excited for me, knowing how much you wanted to be grandparents. We'd be married by now if it weren't for Norman's infection that prevented him from passing the blood test. I caught it from him, but the doctors are positive it won't affect the child.

Although Norm's not well educated, I know that you'll come to accept him as one of our family.

Your loving daughter,
Becky

P.S. There was no fire, I have no concussion, I'm not pregnant, there is no Norman, but I am getting an F in biology, and wanted you to see the grade in proper perspective.[8]

I think that the use of humor in establishing relationships with others is perhaps most clearly exemplified in male social interreactions and bonding. American men use sports and humor as their lingua franca when interacting with other males. Most male conversations start with either a sports score or a joke. According to an article in *Ms.*, a group of men can play poker together for more than twenty years, and they will only know precisely two things about their fellow players: the name of their favorite sports teams and who's the best joke teller in the group. Although *Ms.* has not always been totally accurate and unbiased in its assessment of male behavior, in this instance it was spot-on! Conversations between men almost instantly become either jock talk or joke-offs.[9]

Of course, there are always exceptions to this rule. In my case, it's my best friend, Ron Green. When we meet, Ron never greets me with a joke. Instead, he runs down a list of his latest publications and research projects. (Let us not forget, competition is yet another major ingredient in male camaraderie!) And Ron and I never, ever discuss sports. Ron believes that sports of any kind is a waste of time and energy and is the central cause of the moral and intellectual decline of American society. I, of course, tease him mercilessly on this point. Several years ago, I e-mailed him that I was going to an NFL game between the Chicago Bears and the New York Giants, and I mockingly asked him who he thought would win. Within fewer than five minutes, I received the following response: "I always prefer large hominoids to predatory carnivores! Put your money on the Giants!"

Christopher Hitchens, in his much-maligned and (according to him) misunderstood essay "Why Women Aren't Funny," offers yet other reasons why men tell jokes. Hitchens argues that men do in fact tell more jokes than women and that they, in fact, are better at it. But, he insists, it's not because women aren't funny. Rather, he claims that men need to be funny and therefore are more practiced at humor than women are. To begin with, says Hitchens, male humor arises "from the ineluctable fact that we are all born into a losing struggle." Men, says Hitchens, different from women, instinctively recognize that life is a "joke to begin with, often a joke that has extremely poor taste," and that humor is the "armor plate with which to resist that which is already farcical enough." Second, says Hitchens, lacking in wit, glamour, and good looks, men damn well need to be funny if they hope to impress the opposite sex. Simply put, he claims that men are funnier for Darwinian reasons. That is, males need the gift of humor to persuade women to mate with them.[10]

For Hitchens, humor is not an art form or an attempt to altruistically please or gratify another person. Rather, humor is a sexual strategy motivated by desperation and desire. And yet, when you think about it, even with all the sexist overtones of his argument, isn't Hitchens really talking about someone using humor to reach out to another human being? Isn't he really talking about communication and connectivity, even if the motivation and ultimate purpose of the communication is concupiscence or sexual satisfaction?

Historian Paul Johnson offers us examples of two American presidents who used humor to connect with others and "win friends and influence people": Abraham Lincoln and Ronald Reagan. During the terrible turmoil of the Civil War, Lincoln said, on more than one occasion, that without his jokes, without his stories, without being able to tell a tall tale and laugh, "I would die." And even long before he was president, when he was a traveling lawyer working the trial circuit in central Illinois, Lincoln often used long, complex, parable-like stories about himself to illustrate a point or to win an argument.[11]

My personal favorite Lincoln story is appealing, earthy, and just the kind of folksy thing he would say. Unfortunately, according to Lincoln scholar Paul Zall, although this story is attributed everywhere to Lincoln, there is no definitive proof that Lincoln actually said it.[12] Nevertheless, authentic or apocryphal, the story warrants being retold, and, I think you will agree, it's Lincoln-like and very funny!

A Mississippi River barge rammed the abutment of a newly built railroad bridge spanning the river, causing so much damage that the railroad brought suit to recover. Because the barge's owner questioned the whole right of railroads to interfere with navigation, a battery of high-powered lawyers was imported from the East to present the railroad's case, while the barge owner retained Abraham Lincoln as his sole counsel. The trial was long and tedious, with evidence piled on evidence, but at last the time arrived for the summation speeches by the attorneys. Those for the railroad spoke eloquently, summarizing the evidence, advancing watertight arguments, and clearly impressing the jurors. Then came Lincoln's turn. He rose, strode to the jury box, smiled, and made a single statement: "My learned opponents," he said, "have presented an impressive case. There is no reason to question that they have their facts absolutely right. But they have drawn completely wrong conclusions." The jurors laughed uproariously, adjourned to their deliberations, and after only a few moments returned with a verdict favoring Lincoln's client.

As soon as court adjourned, the railroad attorneys besieged Lincoln with questions. "We had the case won," they told him. "Then you simply tell the jurors that our facts are right and our conclusions wrong, and they decided in your favor. Why? What did you do to them?"

"Well, boys," Lincoln replied, "it just happened that when the court had adjourned for lunch today, I happened into a saloon where the jurors were eating and told them a little story—a story about a farmer who was working in his barnyard one day when his ten-year-old boy came rushing up to him, all excited. 'Paw,' said the boy, 'come quick! The hired man and Sis are up in the hayloft, and he's a-pullin' down his pants, and she's a-liftin' up her skirt. Paw, they're gettin' ready to pee all over our hay.' 'Son,' said the farmer, 'you've got your facts absolutely right, but you've drawn a completely wrong conclusion.'"[13]

Ronald Reagan, the fortieth American president, did not offer long sermons or parables. Rather, he was the master of the one-liner and quick quip. According to historian and journalist Paul Johnson, Reagan used jokes to put people at their ease, to change the mood of the moment, or as a substitute for long arguments or detailed analysis. For example, he once portrayed Washington, DC, as "the only city where sound travels faster than light."[14] And then there was the day Reagan met South African bishop Desmond Tutu in the Oval

Office. Afterward someone asked, "What did you think of Tutu?" Reagan immediately replied, "So-so!"[15]

Reagan reportedly kept a stock of about two thousand one-liners that could be made to fit any situation. He was also able to ad lib like a professional comic even in the most trying of circumstances. On March 30, 1981, Reagan was severely wounded in an assassination attempt in Washington, DC. As he was being wheeled into surgery, he smiled at the anxious-looking doctors and said, "I hope you're all Republicans."[16] Like Lincoln, he was also adept at self-deprecation. He once signed a series of old photos of himself acting with Bonzo the Chimp. Under his signature he added, "I'm the one with the watch." Johnson argues that Reagan used his instincts as a joke teller and called on his training and discipline as a movie star to succeed and survive both as a person and as a president. Reagan once said of himself, "There have been times in this office when I've wondered how you could do the job if you had never been an actor."[17]

DEFENSE MECHANISM

The simple fact of the matter is that life is harsh and fraught with trials and tribulations. Although humor and joke telling are neither a permanent cure nor a direct answer to all of life's challenges, jokes can serve as a temporary reprieve and antidote to the tribulations of life.[18] To paraphrase satirist Christopher Buckley, humor, like alcohol, at least makes our problems and other people momentarily less troublesome.[19]

Humor, deliberate silliness, jokes are benign defense mechanisms that soften the harsh blows of reality and, at least, temporarily put us in control. In his now-classic work *The Act of Creation*, author and journalist Arthur Koestler suggests that humor allows us to view the world through different lenses of our own choosing. It frees the imagination, allowing us to see other possibilities. Laughter offers us a "luxury reflex," which results in double vision.[20] In other words, "We see both the perfect world we desire and the flawed one we live in."[21]

Andrew Hudgins argues that as a species we love to joke and "need to laugh" because there is a "punctuating power to humor." Jokes are weapons made of words. They allow us to take on taboos, poke fun at life, and mock human frailty.[22] Humor, jokes, and laughter can act as both a sword and a shield to defend ourselves against life. At least for a while, humor can detox the mysteries and make the unknown, the intolerable, and the utterly unavoidable more bearable.

In reflecting on the loss of her husband, novelist and essayist Joan Didion reminds us of an obvious and painful truth: "Life changes in an instant, an ordinary instant." The initial and natural way to respond to a tragic event is of course denial, grief, despair, lethargy, and solemn reflection. But, says Didion, hopefully we learn to dwell on other memories and thoughts as well. We can turn to memories of good times, sweet times, humorous times. Even if Didion was not always able to practice what she preached, her insight remains true: humor and laughter can be a bridge between present pain and playful memories.[23]

Friedrich Nietzsche, the German philosopher who, believe me, wasn't a particularly funny type of guy, suggested that to gaze too long into the "gaping abyss" of the unanswerable and unfathomable issues and questions of life leads to despair and futility.[24] I want to argue that humor, laughter, and joke telling are a way to gaze into the abyss, confront the unknowable, and perhaps find comfort and perspective even if no absolute answers are to be found. Humor can offer alternative insights and perspective, some relief from our existential crises and fears, and it can also help us bear the unbearable and deal with the insoluble. Humor allows us to gaze into the abyss and not be defeated. Humor allows us to defang and domesticate our collective fear of what William James, American psychologist and philosopher, calls "the booming, buzzing, confusion of reality."

Freud once said that "humor is a triumph over narcissism."[25] Humor prevents us from perceiving reality as a personal attack or a personal affront. Humor is about the ability to transcend self. It's the ability to celebrate our collective experiences and essential sameness. Humor allows us to laugh at our personal and collective vulnerability. Humor is a celebration of how the frailties of others are also our own. The humorless person is too self-absorbed, too aggressively self-centered, and too myopic to see beyond the needs, wants, and desires of self. Humor has to do with transcending the ambivalence, absurdity, fragility, and nonsense of life. For me, the essence of humor is the ability to laugh both with and at life. It is the ability to appreciate the whimsical, the silly, as well as the absolutely ludicrous and absurdly incongruous aspects of life. It is the ability to step back and be amused, delighted, or surprised by life.

French philosopher André Comte-Sponville argues that humor is a kind of mourning and mocking of the human condition. Humor accepts the human condition as sad and scary and then talks about it, pokes fun at it, laughs at it, and laughs at our feeble responses to it. In so doing, it frees us from dread. It softens the blow of reality. At bottom, humor is a form of "joyful disillusionment"—that is, humor allows us to endure without false illusion or fear the paradoxes and perils of life.[26]

Joking about illness, death, God, sex, or age is a way of defanging or domesticating something that essentially cannot be tamed. It is a way of being in charge of something that we really cannot control or completely understand. Joking about a "deep topic" or "dangerous topic" is a way of talking about it, examining it in a way that doesn't scare us, numb us, and rob us of our joy in life.[27] Jokes allow us to dwell on the incomprehensible without dying from fear or going mad. Laughter and joke telling are a way to speak of the unspeakable. Humor gives us the courage to endure that which we cannot understand or avoid. As the great American philosopher Joan Rivers succinctly put it, "If you can laugh at it, you can live with it."[28]

Mark Twain once said, "Against the assault of laughter, nothing can stand."[29] I agree! Here are a few of my favorite soldiers in my own personal comedic assault against reality.

SEX AND MARRIAGE

A middle-aged married man brags to his best friend, "You know, I've almost had sex every night this week."

"Really?" his friend admiringly replies.

"Yep! I almost had it Monday night. I almost had it Tuesday night. I almost had it Wednesday night . . ."

DEATH

The wife of the deceased is very upset at how her husband looks, and she complains to the mortician. "You have him in a brown suit, and I wanted him in a blue suit," she cries.

"No problem, we'll take care of it," says the mortician. "Yo, Eddie," he yells into the backroom. "Switch the heads on two and four!"

POLITICS

Late one night, a mugger wearing a ski mask jumps into the path of a well-dressed man and stuck a gun in his ribs.

"Give me your money," he demands.

Indignant, the affluent man replies, "You can't do this. I'm a United States congressman!"

"In that case," replies the mugger, "give me back my money."

Aging

Three old men are sitting on the porch of a retirement home. The first says, "Guys, I have real problems. I'm seventy years old. Every morning at seven o'clock I get up and I try to urinate. They give me all kinds of medicine, but nothing helps."

The second old man says, "You think you have problems? I'm eighty years old. Every morning at eight o'clock I get up and try to move my bowels. I try all day long. They give me all kinds of stuff, but nothing helps."

Finally, the third old man speaks up. "Hey, I'm ninety years old. Every morning at seven sharp I urinate. Every morning at eight o'clock I move my bowels. And every morning, bang, at nine, I wake up."

Religion and God

A pastor skips services on Sunday to go bear hunting in the mountains. As he turns the corner along the path, he and a bear collide. The pastor stumbles backward, slips off the trail, and begins tumbling down the mountain, with the bear in hot pursuit. Finally, the pastor crashes into a boulder, sending his rifle flying in one direction and breaking both of his legs. The pastor is lying there, he's lost his gun, and the bear is coming closer. So he cries out in desperation, "Lord, I repent for all I've done. Please make this bear a Christian." The bear skids to halt at the pastor's feet, falls to its knees, clasps its paws together, and says, "Lord, I do thank you for the food I am about to receive."

ILLNESS OR EXISTENTIAL ANGST

Most people think life sucks and then you die. Not me. I beg to differ. I think life sucks; then you get cancer, your dog dies, your wife leaves you, the cancer goes into remission, you get a new dog, you get remarried, you owe ten million dollars in medical bills, but you worked hard for thirty-five years, and then you pay it back, and then one day you have a massive stroke, your whole right side is paralyzed, you have to limp along the streets and speak out of the left side of your mouth and drool, but you go into rehabilitation and regain the power to walk and the power to talk, and then one day you step off a curb at 67th street, and—bang—you get hit by a city bus, and then you die. Maybe! [30]

BUSINESS ETHICS

A father is explaining ethics to his son, who is about to go into business. "Suppose a woman comes in and orders a hundred dollars' worth of material. You wrap it up and give it to her. She pays you with a hundred-dollar bill. But, as she goes out the door, you realize she's given you two hundred-dollar bills. Now, here's where the ethics come in: Should you or should you not tell your business partner?"

Jokes are an attempt to "illuminate the irresolvable contradictions our lives are built on."[31] Humor is an assault on the absurdity, perplexity, and the incomprehensibility of life. Developing a sense of humor, telling jokes, need not be just a flippant attitude we take in regard to life, but is rather a profoundly philosophical way of looking at the world.

Psychiatrist Victor Frankl has pointed out that all too often we cannot change or control the facts of life or the course of our fate, but we can control our attitude with regard to the particular facts of our fate. For me, humor, laughter, and joke telling underlie the attitude I choose to face the irrelevant, the tragic, the absurd, and the overwhelming matters of life that are beyond my control and comprehension. Of course, there is a caveat: humor is not a cure for life, but it can be a helpful temporary anesthesia! I am convinced that laughter demonstrates and reinforces our humanity, encourages hope, and allows us to endure with dignity. Both seriousness and silliness are critical parts of a meaningful life.

Psychologists tell us that laughter reinforces our humanity and defines our individual character.[32] We need to laugh at both the little and the big issues in life in order find balance and moments of peace. Jokes allow us to laugh at the absurdities, complexities, confusions, and the commonness of life.

I believe that laughter is an expression and a defining characteristic of our deepest sense of self. Think about this: What's one of the worst things we can say of another person?

She never told a joke!
She never got a joke!
She never laughs!
She has no sense of humor!

I am also deeply convinced that English poet Samuel Taylor Coleridge was absolutely correct when he said, "People of humor are always in some degree people of genius."[33]

Chapter 4

Dirty Jokes, Tasteless Jokes, Ethnic Jokes

There once was a man from Nantucket
Who kept all his cash in a bucket.
But his daughter, named Nan,
Ran away with a man
And as for the bucket, Nantucket! *

Let's revisit a few basics: Jokes are stories or short narratives based on fiction or fact that are intended to amuse, delight, and possibly inform. Jokes contain a subject and a predicate and very often a direct object. Something is said, something is done, and, more often than not, some*one* is the butt of the story. All jokes are, to some degree or another, edgy, irreverent, iconoclastic. In making fun of somebody or something, jokes push the conventional verbal, conceptual, and cultural envelope. Which means that every joke has the potential to offend someone or to be an affront to something.

Essayist David Galef correctly points out that a joke isn't bad just because it's offensive; every joke risks goring someone's sacred cow. "Language is never neutral," says Galef; it's all about "content and context." The point is, every utterance is a potential slight, but, given the proper context, everything is potentially funny.[1] However, in the wrong context, nothing is funny. Here's an example of a joke that, at first, seems "politically correct" and "totally inoffensive":

> Two men are knocking back beers in a bar on the nine-tieth floor of the Empire State Building.
>
> "You know, there's a slipstream around the seventieth floor," says one, opening a window, "and if you jump out here, it'll suck you back in at the fiftieth floor."
>
> "Ah, c'mon," says the second, more than a little drunk.
>
> "No, really," says the first. "I'll show you." So he jumps out the window, comes in through a fiftieth-floor window, takes the elevator up, and appears triumphantly back in the bar.
>
> "Hey, I'm going to try that," says the second guy. He jumps out the window, falls ninety floors, and is killed instantly.
>
> "Hey," says the bartender, looking hard at the first man, "you can be a real bastard when you're drunk, Superman."[2]

C'mon now, you've got to admit that this is a funny joke! It's got an interesting premise, it's logical, it moves well. And it has an unusual and surprising punch line. So, who can be offended? Superman is not a person! Superman is a fictitious comic book character! True enough, but, as Galef points out, even such a seemingly innocuous joke can prove to be offensive to alcoholics, recovering alcoholics, and families who have suffered pain and loss due to alcoholism. The simple fact is that every utterance has the potential to offend. "Writing or speaking humorously is like playing with matches: it can burn the one who's trying to light up the darkness."[3]

The issue I am pursuing here is not whether a joke is ethically correct or ethically objectionable. We will deal with the ethics of jokes and ethical joke telling in chapter 5. Rather, the issue here is, how is it possible that an utterly tasteless joke—a joke that many consider to be crude, rude, inappropriate, highly offensive, and even harmful—can be considered funny? Remember our four basic elements for comedy from chapter 2? I think that these four ingredients are the keys to our inquiry.

Four Elements of Joke Telling

The Teller	The Joker
The Tale	The Joke
The Timing	The Right Moment
The Told	The Audience

It all starts, of course, with the joker. Like any good salesperson, the joker needs to sell themselves as well as the joke or comedic bit. Whether the joke is delivered by a professional on stage or by a friend over dinner, more often than not jokes succeed or fail depending on how well they are presented. Getting a laugh at a comedy club or at a neighbor's kitchen table is as much a trick of timing, pacing, and delivery as it is a demonstration of true wit.[4] But, in the end, more important than the teller or the timing is the joke itself: the tale only has viability if it has currency with the told. Translation: Does the audience think it's funny? Just as the three ironclad rules of real estate are "Location, Location, Location," a successful joke is all about "Audience, Audience, Audience." The life cycle of a joke is like the physics of sound: a noise must be emitted and received for the circuit to be completed for sound to occur.

Pushed to its logical conclusion, what this means is that nasty jokes, naughty jokes, nefarious jokes, sexual jokes, misogynistic jokes, racial jokes, antireligious jokes, and scatological jokes (no matter how graphic, crude, perverse, despicable, and derogatory) can, depending on the tastes and receptivity of the audience, be considered acceptable fodder for comedy—in other words, be considered funny!

Let's be very clear about this: I'm not talking about jokes that "might" offend Emily Post's refined sensibilities and standards of good taste. Or jokes you probably shouldn't tell your mother. I'm talking about jokes that intentionally, happily, push the limits of sadomasochism. Jokes that far exceed playful childhood scatology. Jokes that are positively gleeful about necrophilia, cannibalism, and torture. Jokes that viciously diminish, denigrate, and defame the basic human rights of various political, racial, or ethnic groups. Jokes that celebrate and advocate violence, mutilation, even death.

No matter how counterintuitive it may seem, a joke that some or many might deem offensive, vulgar, or even unethical doesn't mean that the joke is aesthetically flawed and not funny to a particular audience.[5] As Ted Cohen somewhat reluctantly insists, "Do not let your convictions that a joke is in bad taste, or downright immoral, blind you to whether you find it funny."[6] Ethics, common sense, and good taste aside, the humor of a joke depends "absolutely upon who tells the joke and who hears it."[7]

Let me offer a few rather mild but nonetheless dubious ditties that I think are insensitive, politically incorrect, and perhaps even unethical. Nevertheless, they do have a certain currency with disgruntled former Catholic grammar school students and rabid fans of *Mad Magazine*.

Q: What's black and white and red all over?

A: A crushed nun!

Q: What's that black stuff between an elephant's toes?

A: Slow natives.

A baby seal goes into a bar. The bartender says, "What can I get you to drink, little fellow?" The seal says, "Oh, anything. Just as long as it's not a Canadian Club!"

It is hard to deny that, no matter how tasteless, these jokes contain an element of humor in them. Nevertheless, sharing these jokes with the wrong audience is a guaranteed recipe for comedic failure and social contempt and banishment.

In an interview in the *New York Times Magazine*, comic Jeff Garlin suggests that stand-up comedy is a two-way street. Theoretically, a comedian has a right to tell off-color jokes, antiwomen jokes, rape jokes—any kind of jokes. But when a comedian forgets that there is an audience in front of him, or who his audience is, then, says Garlin, "you're going to pay a price for it." The biggest mistake that any comic can make is to mindlessly assume that the other person's sense of humor is the same as their own.[8] In effect, what Garlin is saying is that, when you do live comedy, the material has to fit the room. The principle of "Audience, Audience, Audience" is absolute and applies to amateurs at open-mike night and seasoned professionals playing to a packed house.

Case in point: the legendary Jerry Seinfeld. Even though his comic persona, for the most part, is studiously apolitical, he has decided to stop working college campus dates. He said that college campuses are now "too PC" and that you have to measure and weigh every word that comes out of your mouth. "It's no fun anymore," says Seinfeld. It takes the pleasure out of doing comedy, and it kills his timing. Even his own college-bound teenage daughter has warned him that he has to watch his language and avoid any words that "might" be construed as racist, sexist, and prejudicial. It's "creepy," said Seinfeld; it "really bothers me." And so he has decided, who needs it? Why bother? I quit![9]

Of course, as *Chicago Tribune* media critic Chris Jones has pointed out, given his power, privilege, and hundreds of millions of dollars, Seinfeld really doesn't need the bother. Besides, as Jones prudently suggested, Seinfeld has a reputation and a legacy to protect. "Seinfeld" is more than just his name; it's the name of a TV show that achieved both popular appeal and critical and academic praise. Legendary comedic stardom and status is difficult to achieve but, oh, so easy to tarnish and lose. Case in point: Bill Cosby.

According to Gershon Legman, underground sexual theoretician and indefatigable encyclopedist of dirty jokes, the most popular form of joke telling is the sex joke. In his magnum opus, *Rationale of the Dirty Joke*, Legman claims that all cultures in all centuries have had an oral and/or written tradition of sexual humor and joke telling. Legman asserts that sexual jokes are part of human culture because sexuality, in all of its varied and peculiar manifestations, is an elemental part of human nature itself.[10]

He claims that we make jokes about sex out of curiosity and as a natural expression of our interest and desire. We tell sex jokes as a way of overcoming our hesitancy and as a way of transcending our fear, neuroses, and guilt in regard to sexual matters. We tell sex jokes to help normalize an otherwise forbidden—or at least hidden—topic. We tell sex jokes as a way of flaunting authority, as a means of transcending cultural conventions, and as a means of violating taboos. Sexual jokes are also a way to express illicit sexual rage and perversions of every kind. Sexual joke making is a means of compensating for that which is unavailable to us in reality. And, lest we forget, sexual jokes, like pornography, are also a vicarious means of experiencing sexual pleasure.

The spectrum of the tone, taste, patterns of aggression, and ferocity of the language and imagery involved in sexual joke telling is rather amazing. Erotic jokes range from guarded and subdued to poignantly pornographic, violent, and explicit. Linguistically, most (but not all) erotic jokes traffic heavily in profane language. Profane language is considered irreverent language. Profane language is considered vulgar, common, dirty language. But as comedian George Carlin (1937–2008) asked of his various audiences, "Can someone explain to me why certain words are considered dirty? Why is it that of the four hundred thousand–plus words in the English language, seven of them (S____, P___, F___, C___, C____ S_____, M_____F_____, and T___) are thought to be too dirty and improper to use on TV and in most newspapers? None of these words," said Carlin, will "infect your soul, curve your spine, and keep the country from winning [a] war."[11]

In 1972 Carlin performed his "Seven Dirty Words" routine in Milwaukee and was arrested for violating obscenity laws. In 1973 a New York radio station got into hot water with the Federal Communications Commission for playing Carlin's monologue on air. The case wound up in the Supreme Court. In 1978 the court upheld the government's right to penalize radio and TV stations that broadcast "indecent" materials on public airwaves during prime-time hours (6 a.m. to 10 p.m.) when young people typically tune in. In the present world of cable broadcasting and the Internet, this ruling now seems quaintly medieval or something akin to the Salem witch trials of 1692. Today, in the words of Cole Porter, "Anything goes!" The world of cable and cyberspace is now awash in naughty words, complete nudity, and explicit sex.

Fellow dirty-mouthed comedian Lewis Black is in complete agreement with Carlin's original comic premise. Language, says Black, is a tool and a means of communication. And, Black goes on, we use different kinds of language to express ourselves differently. He asks, "When you're watching a body of water rise up and crush everything in its path, don't words like 'Son of a Bitch' or 'Holy Shit' cross your mind? Does anyone really think, 'Aw, Pshaw' or 'Pussy feathers'??" In the same way, says Black, a "good dirty joke" needs "good, dirty language."[12]

But, warns Black, you don't get laughs just by swearing. After the first few times you've heard them, four-letter words in and of themselves are not funny. On stage, just saying "dick" or "fuck" is not going to get you a laugh. To get a laugh, you've got to develop and deliver some quality "dick" and "fuck" jokes. In other words, comedy is about the joke; the language is just a colorful and playful delivery system.[13] Says Black, "When you are not delivering the goods"—a good joke—"all the 'fucks' in the world won't save your ass."[14] Conversely, it can be argued that, if the joke is a good one, then there is no limit to the range and raunchiness of the language and the number of times the

F-bomb or bad language is used. The classic case in point is the infamous joke "The Aristocrats."

Arguably, "The Aristocrats" is the dirtiest joke in the English language. According to Gershon Legman, its origin dates back to the vaudeville and burlesque days of show business, and the joke has long been recognized as the benchmark of grossness and sexual excess in the extreme. Today, "The Aristocrats" is rarely performed on stage, but it continues to be told by comics to other comics both as a way of demonstrating professional competence and as a form of competitive one-upmanship. According to Penn Jillette and Paul Provenza, who produced and directed the 2005 documentary *The Aristocrats*, the joke is now an insider's joke, exclusively told by professionals to professionals. The joke has become an "acid test of talent, wit, and unflinching nerve, of who can out-cringe whom."[15]

The skeleton of the joke is simplicity itself. There is a standard opening setup: "A man walks into the office of a well-known talent agent and says, 'Sir, have I got an act for you . . . It's a family act!'" The middle of the joke is a blank slate and offers an opportunity for the gleeful expression of the obscene and perverted imagination of each individual comedian. There is but one rule: "unspeakable obscenity" is to be spoken here! No topic, no form of language, no gesture, no matter how disgusting, is out of bounds. The goal of the joke is to achieve "shock and awe!" And so every version of the joke must, by tradition, be an outrageous depiction of sexual depravity, ranging from bestiality to pedophilia to you-name-it. And, finally, the joke ends with the rather unexpected punch line: "We call ourselves . . . The Aristocrats!"

In the documentary, over one hundred different comics joyfully share their version of the joke with the viewing audience and their fellow comics. Each version is deliciously decadent, sexually outrageous, and uncomfortably frank, but, nevertheless, hysterically funny. Unfortunately, good taste, professional prudence, and the advice of my attorney prevent me from sharing with you a full version of "The Aristocrats." Nevertheless, allow me to offer a fill-in-the-blank version of the joke—sans vulgarity and graphic sexuality. Feel free to try your hand at what the *New Yorker* calls not just the "dirtiest joke in the English language" but also "the filthiest joke in the world."[16]

The Aristocrats

A man walks into the office of a well-known talent agent and says, "Sir, have I got an act for you."

The agent, having seen it all in his forty years in the business, looks doubtful but indicates that the man should go on.

"Well, sir," the man says, "it's a family act." The agent rolls his eyes, but, before he can respond, the man jumps right in. "First," he says, "I come out on the stage and am accompanied by an old-time piano rag, do a bit of soft-shoe dance. My wife joins me, and I take her by the hand. Then I bend her over, lift up her _____ [article of clothing] and tear off her _____ [article of clothing].

Next, I whip out my _____ [body part] and start to _____ [verb] her. As she's _____ [verb ending in –ing] with pleasure, my son comes onstage and pulls out his little _____ [body part], which my wife starts to _____ [verb]. After a moment, our daughter enters from the left, kneels down, and starts licking the boy's _____ [body part]. Overcome with pleasure, he _____ [verb ending in –s], and some lands on our daughter's _____ [body part]. All the while, the music is playing, becoming more and more dramatic. Then, the baby crawls onstage, in her adorable footie pajamas, and starts to eat the _____ [bodily waste] right off her sister's _____ [body part]. The baby _____ [verb ending in –s], and my daughter slips in the ensuing puddle. Her face gets caught in the boy's _____ [body part], and my wife, still _____ [verb ending in –ing] away on his _____ [body part], tries to pull the two of them apart. Off balance, she slips and lands face-first in the steaming pile of _____ [noun]. The motion of her popping off my _____ [body part], along with the music rising to a mighty crescendo, causes me to _____ [verb] all over them, while they slip and slide in the _____ [noun], which by now is covering the stage. Just at that moment, a container of confetti opens up in the rafters, and my entire family gets up and leaps on top of my shoulders, fanning out like the petals of a flower, with the baby perched on top. Finally," the man says, "when we're all completely covered in _____

[noun], _____ [bodily fluid], and confetti, we throw our hands in the air: Ta-da!"

The agent, stunned, pauses for what seems like an eternity before saying, "Jesus, that's a hell of an act. What do you call it?"

The man, rubbing his fingernails on the lapel of his natty, pin-striped jacket, lifts his nose to the air and says, in his most sophisticated voice, "We call ourselves . . . The Aristocrats!"[17]

Ironically, in the end, "The Aristocrats" may be funny not just because it is shockingly salacious and uncomfortably prurient but also because it is outrageously bombastic and iconoclastic. The joke itself is tasteless and absurd, and it is this very absurdity that makes it hilarious. Added to that (at least in regard to the documentary) is the energy and excitement of the comics acting out and performing the piece. In some sense, "The Aristocrats" is as much a dramatic farce as it is a joke.

By way of an aside, having defended the richness, if not the purity, of dirty jokes and the use of bad language, I'd like to offer my two favorite sex jokes. You will notice that nary a naughty word is to be found in either of these jokes. There is absolutely no use of Carlin's seven forbidden sexual terms or even any explicit description of sex. Nonetheless, the setups and the punch lines of the jokes following are undeniably sexual, naughty, and funny.

Genie in the Bottle

A retired Jewish man is walking on the beach when he sees a bottle in the sand. He picks it up and rubs it, and a genie comes out. The genie promises to grant him one wish.

The man says, "Ah, peace in the Middle East—that's my wish."

The genie looks concerned, then says, "I'm sorry, sir. I come from the Middle East myself, and these conflicts have been raging since even before my time. Bringing peace to that region is beyond my powers. Do you have another wish?"

The guy thinks and says, "Well, I've been married for forty years, and in my whole life I've never received oral sex from my wife. That would be my wish."

The genie pauses for another moment and then says, "Hm . . . So, tell me, how exactly would you define peace?"

Bear Hunting

Bob was excited about his new .338 rifle and decided to try bear hunting. He traveled up to Alaska, spotted a small brown bear, and shot it. Soon after there was a tap on his shoulder, and he turned around to see a big black bear.

The black bear said, "That was a very bad mistake. That bear was my cousin. I'm going to give you two choices: either I maul you to death or we have sex."

After considering briefly, Bob decided to accept the latter alternative. So the black bear had his way with Bob.

Even though he felt sore for two weeks, Bob soon recovered and vowed revenge. He headed out on another trip to Alaska, where he found the black bear and shot it dead. Right after, there was another tap on his shoulder. This time a huge grizzly bear stood right next to him.

The grizzly said, "That was a big mistake, Bob. That bear was my cousin, and you've got two choices: either I maul you to death or we have rough sex."

Again, Bob thought it was better to cooperate with the grizzly bear than be mauled to death. So the grizzly had his way with Bob.

Although he survived, it took several months before Bob fully recovered. Now Bob was completely outraged, so he headed back to Alaska and managed to track down the grizzly bear and shot it. He felt sweet revenge, but then, moments later, there was a tap on his shoulder. He turned around to find a giant polar bear standing there.

The polar bear looked at him and said, "Admit it, Bob—you don't come here just for the hunting, do you?"

ETHNIC JOKES

Ethnic humor is another area of joke telling where, like it or not, anything goes. Depending on the teller, the tale, and to whom the joke is being told, ethnic and racial jokes can prove to be either delightful and delicious or dehumanizing and disgusting. And, unfortunately, riffing on the words of philosopher Thomas Hobbes, ethnic jokes too often prove to be nasty, brutish, cruel, stereotypical, and demeaning. But I want to point out that good ethnic humor need not and should not be this way.

It can be argued that ethnic humor evolves out of our natural tendency to compare and measure ourselves against others. As a species, we are a competitive group, and we revel in the opportunity to laugh at people not like us—and at others whom we regard as dim-witted or peculiar or simply different in their customs and habits.[18] So, for example, the English laugh at the French, the Belgians deride the Dutch, the Swedes scorn the Danes, the Chinese cackle about the Japanese, the Democrats disparage the Republicans, and, in the National Football League, the Chicago Bears defame the Green Bay Packers—and vice versa, of course. Some of these comparisons are clever, and many are cruel. Here's an example of one that is right down the middle.

The Greeks versus the Italians

A Greek and an Italian were debating who has the superior culture.

The Greek says, "We have the Parthenon."

The Italian says, "We have the Colosseum."

The Greek says, "We had great mathematicians and philosophers."

The Italian says, "We created a world empire and established Pax Romana."

And so on and so on, for hours, until finally the Greek lights up and says, "We invented sex!"

The Italian nods slowly, thinks, and replies, "That is true—but it was Italians who introduced it to women."

A lot of ethnic humor sarcastically plays on certain long-established and popularly recognized cultural traits and particular idiosyncrasies of a group or ethnicity. Many of these kinds of jokes are more playful than negative or derogatory. For example,

Q: How did the Irish jig get started?

A: Too much Guinness and not enough bathrooms!

Q: What do you call it when an Italian has one arm shorter than the other?

A: A speech impediment!

Q: What goes CLOP, CLOP, CLOP, BANG, BANG, BANG, CLOP, CLOP, CLOP?

A: An Amish drive-by shooting.

Q: What do you get when you cross a Unitarian with a Jehovah's Witness?

A: Someone out knocking on doors for no apparent reason.

Next to the pleasure that many of us derive from making fun of others, the origin of much of ethnic humor is self-generated—that is, we love to make fun of ourselves. Most, but not all, ethnic groups have created a treasure trove of self-referential stories, anecdotes, and jokes that examine and celebrate their collective habits, customs, and peculiarities in both their adopted communities and their countries of origin. Sociologists contend that much of ethnic humor and storytelling comes out of the experience of migrating to new lands and becoming linguistically and ethnically the "outsider." According to folklorist James P. Leary, developing a strong culture of humor and storytelling within immigrant or ethnic groups allows the group to hold onto the past while being in the present. In effect, says Leary, humor allows them to be "bicultural." It allows them to overcome the malaise of being "strangers in a strange land." Self-deprecating and self-referential jokes becomes the language of assimilation and integration while still retaining some of the manners and morals of the old world. Their jokes afford them the status of being both insiders and outsiders.[19]

Leary and other students of ethnic humor are quick to point out that the key to ethnic humor is not always the old-world content of the joke as much as the tone, topics, language, and delivery of the joke. In Wisconsin and Minnesota, for example, Ole and Lena are stars of local Scandinavian humor. The longtime host of NPR's *Prairie Home Companion*, Garrison Keillor, is a big fan of Ole and Lena jokes. According to Keillor, Ole and Lena are not "simple";

rather, they are people of simple values and a parochial lifestyle. They're rural people—farmers and laborers. They've been in the Midwest for generations, but they still speak "Scand-lish," and their humor is dry, prosaic, prudential, and never over-the-top.

Anniversary Party

Ole and Lena were celebrating their twenty-fifth anniversary. After the guests left, Lena looked at Ole and punched him real hard in the shoulder. "That's for twenty-five years of bad sex."

Ole thought about it, and then he reached over and punched Lena hard in her shoulder. "That's for knowing the difference!"

Death Scene

Ole was dying. On his deathbed, he looked up and said, "Is my wife here?"

Lena replied, "Yes, Ole, I'm here, next to you."

So Ole asked, "Are my children here?"

"Yes, Daddy, we're all here," said the children.

"Are my other relatives also here?"

And they said, "Yes, we are all here."

Ole asked, "Then why is the light on in the kitchen?"

Sam Hoffman, connoisseur of Hebrew humor and author of the play and book *Old Jews Telling Jokes*, points out that, by and large, Jewish folk humor is urban, urbane, about being the chosen people, and about "making a living." And, of course, there are lots of jokes about Jewish mothers. According to Hoffman, for generations Jewish mothers have occupied a central role in Jewish culture. Traditionally, Jewish mothers run the household, keep a laser-like focus on the children, participate in the life of the synagogue, and keep their husbands on the straight and narrow. And how do these extraordinary women accomplish all of this? Simple, says Hoffman: with huge doses of nagging and lots and lots of guilt![20]

The following are my all-time favorite Jewish-mother jokes. To me, they capture the essence of Jewish-mother jokes: whining, nagging, and the not-so-subtle communication, from mother to child, that "nothing is ever good enough!"

The year is 2020, and the United States has elected the first woman as well as the first Jewish president, Susan Goldfarb. She calls up her mother a few weeks after Election Day and says, "So, Mom, I assume you'll be coming to my inauguration?"

"I don't think so. It's a ten-hour drive, your father isn't as young as he used to be, and my arthritis is acting up again."

"Don't worry about it, Mom—I'll send Air Force One to pick you up and take you home. And a limousine will pick you up at our door."

"I don't know. Everybody will be so fancy-schmancy; what on earth would I wear?"

Susan replies, "I'll make sure you have a wonderful gown custom-made by the best designer in New York."

"Honey," Mom complains, "you know I can't eat those rich foods you and your friends like to eat."

The president-elect responds, "Don't worry, Mom. The entire affair is going to be handled by the best caterer in New York—kosher all the way. Mom, I really want you to come."

So her mother reluctantly agrees, and on January 20, 2021, Susan Goldfarb is sworn in as president of the United States. In the front row sits the new president's mother, who leans over to a senator sitting next to her and says, "You see that woman over there with her hand on the Torah, becoming president of the United States?"

The senator whispers back, "Yes, I do."

Mom says proudly, "Her brother is a doctor."

Harold Leibowitz excitedly tells his mother he's fallen in love and that he is going to get married. He says, "Just for fun, Mom, I'm going to bring over three women, and you try to guess which one I'm going to marry."

The mother agrees.

The next day, Harold brings three beautiful women into the house and sits them down on the couch, and they chat for a while. He then says, "Okay, Mother, guess which one I'm going to marry."

The mother says immediately, "The one on the right."

"That's amazing, Mom! You're right. How did you know?"

She replies, "Because her I don't like."

Sadly and unfortunately, there is a special codicil to the basic thesis that joke telling helps one navigate a hostile or new environment. During World War II, the Nazi regime attempted to carry out a plan—a "final solution"—for the complete extermination of European Jewry. Millions of Jews were packed into cattle cars and shipped off to concentration and death camps. Once there, prisoners were either selected for immediate extermination or forced into an inhumane work environment without sufficient clothing, food, or opportunities for rest. Numerous survivors of the Holocaust—the Shoah—have reported on the unrelenting horror and cruelty of the experience. Twelve to fourteen hours of work on fewer than eight hundred calories of food a day. A daily selection of those chosen to die next. The ever-present stench of burning flesh in the air, and the ubiquitous cloud of gray ash that spewed forth from the incinerator chimneys. Clearly it was a twentieth-century version of Dante's third circle of Hell.

One of the most famous survivors of the camps was psychiatrist and philosopher Viktor Frankl. Frankl lost most of his family in the camps and endured almost four years of hard labor at Auschwitz. In his deeply disturbing, yet profoundly moving, book, *Man's Search for Meaning*, Frankl reports that he learned four essential life lessons while enduring the horrors of camp life. To begin with, he found out that the medical community was wrong: the human body can cope with far more torture, pain, cold, sleep deprivation, and starvation than what the medical textbooks claimed. Second, even in the face of the senseless, arbitrary cruelty, we have a nagging need to find meaning and purpose in our lives: "To live is to suffer," said Frankl, "to survive is to find meaning in the suffering."[21] Third, forces beyond our control can take away everything we possess except one thing—our freedom to choose how we will respond to the conditions that we face.[22] Finally, he learned that humor "affords us an aloofness and ability to rise above any situation, even if only for a few seconds. . . . I would never have made it," said Frankl, "if I could not have laughed. Laughing lifted me momentarily . . . out of this horrible situation, just enough to make it livable . . . survivable."[23] And, as another famous inmate, Eugène Ionesco, put it, "To become conscious of what is horrifying and to laugh at it is to become master of that which is horrifying."[24]

It's certainly not the case that prisoners in these concentration camps greeted each other at roll call by saying, "Hey, did you hear the one about . . . ?" Nor did they sit over their eight ounces of rancid gruel each night and swap nasty and satirical Nazi stories. Rather, said Frankl, inmates tried to use their imagination to create or see humor in any situation possible. For example, there is the story of a prisoner who points to a particularly severe and sadistic capo (a trustee, a prisoner who served as guard) and ironically says, "Imagine! I knew him when he was only the president of a bank!"[25]

What follows are a few more frequently repeated stories that came out of the concentration camps:

> A prisoner bumps into a guard. The guard shouts at him, "*Schwein* [pig]!" The prisoner bows and says, "Cohen. Pleased to meet you."

> Martha is standing next to Sarah during the daily roll call and says to her, "You look good! Have you lost a little weight?"

> Two prisoners are waiting to face a firing squad, when news arrives that they are to be hanged instead. One turns to the other and says, "You see, they must be losing the war because they are running out of ammunition!"[26]

> A prisoner wanted to commit suicide and tried hanging himself. But the quality of the rope in the noose was so bad that it broke. So he tried sticking his head in the oven, but they shut off the gas between two and five in the afternoon. Then he tried living on his rations. That worked like a charm.[27]

German historian Rudolph Herzog maintains that these kinds of jokes are an expression of the Jewish prisoner's desire to survive against all odds. Such jokes are a desperate attempt to deny, if only momentarily, the everyday terror of the camps. For Herzog, these jokes are an act of defiance: "My back is to the wall, [but] I'm still laughing." These jokes are proof that I'm not dead yet: "I laugh, therefore I am!"[28] To laugh in the face of absurdity does not negate the absurdity, but somehow it becomes, at least briefly, just a bit more bearable.[29]

In the end, I think ethnic jokes are small anthropological essays,[30] little ethnic homilies that give us a perspective on our own cultural traditions and the practices of others. I think that the beauty and the larger purpose of ethnic humor is that it shows up our similarities more than our differences. It makes us aware of how much we are alike and how much we share. To me, a good ethnic joke is really a folk tale, a piece of folk wisdom about something that crosses ethnic and racial lines. It can be argued, for example, that a Jewish joke, an Italian joke, or a Greek joke about a mother is really a story about all mothers everywhere and probably applies to many, but not necessarily all, ethnic groups.

To help prove my point, fill in the following blanks with the ethnicity of your choice.

Q: How many [____] mothers does it take to screw in a light bulb?

A: Don't bother! It's all right! Don't worry about me! I'll just sit here in the dark!

Q: What's the difference between a [____] mother and a pit bull dog?

A: Sooner or later, the dog lets go!

Proof positive that Jesus was [_____]:

1. He lived at home until he was thirty.
2. The night before he died, he went out drinking with his buddies.
3. His mother thought he was God.
4. He thought his mother was a virgin.

A son, calls his [_____] mother in Florida.

SON: Hi, Mom! How are you?

MOM: Not too good; I've been weak.

SON: Why have you been weak?

MOM: Never mind.

SON: Mom, what's wrong?

MOM: It's okay, don't worry.

SON: Stop this! Tell me, what's wrong?

MOM: All right, I haven't eaten in thirty-eight days.

SON: That's terrible! Why haven't you eaten in thirty-eight days?

MOM: Because I didn't want my mouth to be filled with food if you should finally call!

Anthropologically speaking, jokes can help break down stereotypes and displace and disarm our fear and discomfort in regard to our dealings with others. Comically speaking, I think that most ethnic jokes speak to the very core of what humor is about: making light of and laughing at life. Folk tales, stories, and jokes may not be the answer to all of life's problems, but they can be a balm and offer genuine, if only temporary, comfort.

Whatever the joke, whatever the topic, whatever the level of depravity, whatever the level of lewd, lecherous, sexual raunchiness, whatever the ethnic or racial vitriol of a joke, and no matter how decadent or déclassé, someone, some audience, might relate to it, might take some comfort in it, and might think it funny. Just ask Southern humorist and stand-up comic Jeff Foxworthy.

> If you go to family reunions to pick up girls, guess what? You just might be a redneck!

> If your daddy walks you to school because you're both in the same grade, guess what? You just might be a redneck!

Jokes such as these, jokes that celebrate being a redneck—"a person who suffers from a glorious absence of sophistication"—propelled Mr. Foxworthy into the natural spotlight. And thanks to a number of TV shows, eleven *New York Times* best-selling books, and twenty award-winning and best-selling comedy albums, his personal net worth is estimated to be in excess of $100 million. Ain't comedy grand??

Okay, so naughty, salacious, racial, homophobic misanthropic, misogynous jokes may in fact, counterintuitively, be funny. Now we need to ask the question: Are they ethical?

CHAPTER 5

A Conversation with a Colleague about Humor and Ethics

I've been accused of vulgarity. I say that's bullshit!
—MEL BROOKS

Joke telling, like language, is never a game of solitaire; it's always a shared, gregarious experience. One has to be part of a community, tribe, or group for communication to occur. Jokes that cannot find an audience are dead. Or, more accurately, they are not jokes at all. And no matter how disgusting, raunchy, disturbing, or salacious a particular joke may be, given the right audience, it can be funny. But now we face a larger and more important question: Even when you have a receptive, open-minded, or similarly minded audience, how do we decide if a particular joke is ethical or unethical? Even when the audience thinks it's funny, how do we decide if the joke should be told at all?

Case in point: the reigning princess of comedy, Amy Schumer. In 2015 she was heavily criticized for using her seemingly innocent, attractive, cute, white, blonde, starry-eyed, "Daddy's precious baby" persona as her comedic cover and setup for the following joke: "I used to date Latino guys, but now I prefer consensual [sex]!" At the time, Schumer was vilified in the press and on social media. But she casually tossed off most of the flak that she was receiving. She seemed irritated more than angry or outraged by the pushback. Her arguments in response to the criticism were rather straight-forward: (1) "I'm saying dumb stuff to make a larger point." (2) "In making racial jokes, I'm trying to say race no longer matters because we've transcended it." (3) "It's a joke, and it's funny. . . . I am not going to start joking about safe material!"[1]

Personally, I think Amy Schumer is a brilliant stand-up comedian and an extremely talented comic writer. Witness her successful Emmy Award–winning Comedy Central TV show, *Inside Amy Schumer*, her runaway 2015 movie box office hit *Train Wreck*, and the $8,000,000 advance she received for her first book of essays, *The Girl with the Lower Back Tattoo*. But the fact is, at best, her "dating joke" is edgy and insensitive, except *perhaps* if it were told by a Latina comic to an all-Hispanic audience. At worst, the joke is downright unethical, no matter who is telling it, and no matter the makeup of the audience.

For a lot of people, comedy simply transcends the usual cultural and moral norms. "C'mon," people will say, "it's just a joke." Or "Calm down—jokes let us cross the line on any issue." In theory, in a perfect world, yes. But as Emily Nussbaum of the *New Yorker* has noted, the phrase "Can't you take a joke?" is too often code for the justification of sexism, racism, or the expression of any prejudicial point of view of your choosing. "It's just a joke" can be used as a flimsy excuse to justify perhaps technically funny but nevertheless unethical jokes about rape, race, homophobia, misogyny, and so on.[2]

Many people also claim that joke telling is cathartic and can disarm and dismantle various stereotypes and prejudices and level the playing field for all concerned. But . . . not always. In fact, I would argue that it is "virtually impossible to make a joke about racism or sexism that isn't also a racist sexist joke."[3] Ironically, in trying to "defang" a sensitive topic, joking can inadvertently normalize and entrench racism, or any prejudicial point of view, rather than neutralize or negate it. The danger in telling funny racist or sexist jokes is that we run the risk of perpetrating the negative ideas that they reflect. As Aristotle suggested over 2,300 years ago in *Poetics*, comedy can be a "species of the ugly."[4]

More recently, Steve Martin pointed out that "comedy is not pretty."[5] But he meant something quite different from what Aristotle was alluding to. I think that Martin means that comedy is a stick we can use to poke at something painful or something that we dislike. Comedy can disarm and domesticate our fears and our discomfort. Comedy can be boisterous, biting, iconoclastically satirical, shocking, off-putting, and probing. But it need not, and should not, be degrading, derogatory, or dehumanizing. It need not be personally "ugly." It need not be poignantly unethical.

The problem is that, whenever anyone brings up the topic of ethics, eyes begin to glaze over, people will excuse themselves from the conversation, and someone will invariably try to change the subject. In fact, ethics is not abstruse or abstract or as complicated as astrophysics. Nor is it as gory as brain surgery or as mysteriously medieval as the question "How many angels can dance on the heard of a pin?" (By the way, the correct answer to that question is seven! Or nine, if a couple of the angels are anorexic.) Ethics is nothing more than the study of the quality of our interactions with others and the rights and obligations that we have and share with others. Ethics is the recognition of the "brute fact" that we are not alone—and that we are not the center of the universe. Ethics is primarily a communal pursuit, not a solitary one. It is the study of our web of relations with others. Ethics is the attempt to rationally work out how we ought to live with others. Ethics is about civility, courtesy, politeness, fairness, and justice in our relations and treatment of others. In some sense, it can be argued that ethics is a series of commonsensical, practical guidelines for living with others. As theologian Frank Griswold so eloquently phrased it, "Ethics is about the rules we chose to live by once we decide we want to live together."[6]

Living together and living well with others requires us to develop cooperative behaviors and habits that demonstrate our recognition and concern for others—habits that are kind, convivial, and not off-putting. Habits that breed cooperation, camaraderie, and community. One such habit is the practice of making people happy, making people laugh, telling them a joke. Although it is sage advice to "shun the buffoon whose joke making is excessive and off-putting," when told in moderation, jokes are an attempt to be kind and a demonstration of our shared humanity. Jokes are an attempt to reach out and commiserate with others.

I think that having a sense of humor is a talent, a gift, and a virtue. The Greek word for virtue is *areté*. It literally means "excellence." Virtues are desirable traits of character that we choose to make second nature by repetition and habit. Virtuous habits are not an accident, mere luck, or a one-time event. A virtuous act is doing the right thing for the right reason, habitually and purposefully. A person of courage, generosity, moderation, truthfulness, and (I would add) humor is better able to achieve the Greek ideal state of *eudaimonia*, usually translated as "happiness," "flourishing," or "the good life."

I am convinced that jokes and joke telling can be seen as a virtuous act, an ethical act. Telling jokes at the right time and place is a kindness, an attempt to be of comfort to others. Jokes are a *bonum delectabile*—"a pleasurable good"—a good thing in itself. Jokes can be a way of reaching out, offering solidarity, and being empathic to the needs of others. In the words of best-selling author Norman Cousins, "When we laugh with others, we feel more connected with them in the world."[7] I am convinced that we must also be able to laugh *at* ourselves and *with* others. I believe the "sanity of self" requires a playful appreciation of the incongruity and incomprehensibility of life. Humor is a necessary ingredient in the ethical equation of learning to live with others. We need to laugh. We want to laugh. Jokes help make life bearable. Jokes help us endure. Therefore I would argue that humor is a requirement of life. In fact, I would argue that we have an obligation, a duty, a Comedic Imperative, to practice and share humor, laughter, and jokes with others. But we must always be mindful of the admonition that "nothing shows a person's true character more than what he or she laughs at." Unethical humor that deprecates and denigrates others diminishes both the teller and the told; it both insults and isolates us from one another.

To add another voice to this conversation, and to pursue this rather complex topic in greater depth and with greater perspective, I call on my friend Ron Green. I have already introduced you to Ron as the man who loathes and despises sports of all kinds. While that might be true, Ron is a connoisseur of comedy, a devotee of the arts, and an internationally recognized scholar in ethics. His credentials include serving as the director of Dartmouth's Ethics Institute, chair of the Department of Religious Studies, and author or editor of fourteen books and more than 170 articles on the topics of ethics, philosophy, and religion. Digital recorder at the ready, and with each of us wearing our own personal pair of Groucho Marx black-framed glasses (complete with fake nose and mustache), I cornered Ron in his Cape Cod hideaway and bombarded him with questions about comedy, joke telling, and ethics. Here are just a few of his responses.

RON: Let me start off by saying that I'm not sure if I want to completely agree that humor is a virtue and that we have a moral obligation to use and be open to humor in our interactions with others. While I believe that humor and joke telling is part of the equation of living well with others, I do not think that it is an absolute obligation.

Humor, I agree, is something that enhances human life, and it is something that most people want to experience in their personal relationships and society at large. In this sense, it is an excellent quality or talent like athletic grace or musical ability. It is good, excellent, to possess these kinds of attributes or talents, but they are not morally necessary. I want to argue that humor is a gift, a talent, a skill, but it is not a moral virtue in the sense that you are claiming. Nor do I think that we have an ethical obligation to cultivate humor. I say this for a very simple reason: a person can be a fine, upstanding individual in every way but neither tell nor appreciate jokes. In fact, I have two friends whom I admire in every way for their private and public virtues. Yet neither has a sense of humor. They're poker-faced when jokes are told, and they never tell a joke themselves. (It happens that both are Canadians. Are we learning something here?) This said, I fully grant that humor is an important ingredient in our lives. And I will also admit that humor, used well and appropriately, is a vital social asset.

AL: Can you develop what you exactly mean by referring to humor as a social asset?

RON: Besides offering delight and distraction, I think that humor can help disassemble and deconstruct the status quo. Humor is able to penetrate and deflate arrogance and pride by poking fun at our acquired cultural conceits and our unexamined social practices and habits. Humor has the ability to unpack and expose the inner logic of our social rules and codes of conduct. It can detox and take the edge off of reality. It can offer comfort by confronting and combating conventional wisdom. Humor can be a catalyst for reexamination and renewal. It can be both an act of defiance and a buffer against absurdity and fear. I'm not denying the significant role of humor in our lives; what I question is your claim that each of us has a moral obligation to develop our sense of humor.

AL: I recently came across a quote from Friedrich Nietzsche that I would like you to comment on: "We have art in order to not die from the truth."

RON: Well, if we substitute the word *humor* for *art*, isn't this exactly what we're both thinking about but in a slightly different way? I think we both agree that humor is an "asset," a method, or a means of approaching topics and issues that are impenetrable, unresolvable, unavoidable, and more than a little frightening to us all. To borrow one of your phrases, isn't Nietzsche suggesting that humor can, like art, at least for a little while, "defang our fears" and deescalate our anxieties about life?

What Nietzsche is suggesting is that to live is to suffer and that art and humor make that suffering less fearsome and less crippling. In spite of the fact that life is ultimately about decay, loss, and death, we all seek and need moments of joy, pleasure, and hope. Humor, like art, can help us dull the pain and offer us the least momentary reprieve.

There's an old cartoon that, I think, nicely captures the spirit of Nietzsche's quote. The cartoon is a depiction of a cemetery and headstone. The inscription reads, "Jacob Abraham Goldberg: 1912–1982. Never sick a day in his life, and now . . . this!" For me, at least, the lesson here is both obvious and painfully funny: Even though his health was good, there's no escaping death. It's our fate. But, at least for a moment, this rather absurd piece of art, that we call a joke, allows us an escape from the pain and terror of the inevitable. To paraphrase the words of one of my favorite comics, Louis C.K., what comedy is really good at is its ability to take people to the scariest part of their minds and somehow make it less scary.

AL: Jokes can be vicious or virtuous. Can the phrase "It's just a joke!" be used as a pardon or passport that allows a comedian to say anything, as long as it's presented as being an attempt to be funny?

RON: No! Telling a joke is not a get-out-of-jail card that lets you say anything that you want to say. "You just didn't get it" is never a sufficient or a satisfactory excuse to justify or explain away a malevolent or vicious comedic zinger! The use of humor does not disengage or detach us from our basic responsibilities and relationships with others. To intentionally laugh at or callously ridicule the misfortunes of others—to laugh about who they are, the color of their skin or their particular personal circumstances—is reprehensible, destructive, and unethical.

AL: So, is there a specific "comedic code" that determines what's good or bad, acceptable or unacceptable, when it comes to joke telling?

RON: Yes, there is. And it's easy to state, but, due to the absurdity and iconoclastic nature of comedy, it is oftentimes difficult to make a clear judgment about the ethical status of a joke. For example, the Amy Schumer joke: Is she trying to defend or deny the point of the joke? Can't it be argued, as she does, that her cute, clownish delivery of the joke, in fact, satirically deconstructs and belittles the punch line? Might she be correct that the joke is an attempt to deflate and negate a cultural stereotype?

The problem with this joke, and many other "edgy" jokes, is that a moral judgment has to be made. And all moral judgments are nuanced, complex, and must take into account the situation, the participants involved, and the intent of the actor. It's not always easy to figure that all out.

The rules for ethical joke telling is a balancing act between *who's* telling the joke, *who's* hearing the joke, and *who's* the joke about. But, again, although the determining standard of right and wrong is simple to state, it is often difficult to adjudicate the issue. Is the joke unnecessarily hurtful, hateful, demeaning, or destructive? Are particular individuals or groups being viciously stereotyped, unjustly vilified, or maliciously defamed? If so, then the joke should be considered unethical and not be told.

I know that a big part of the equation for judging humor is audience, audience, audience, but I'm convinced that you shouldn't tell a demeaning or vicious joke even to an audience of highly responsive, howling bigots! Once again, to use some of your language, the bottom line for me is that unethical jokes wind up wounding and harming both the teller and the told and therefore shouldn't be told.

AL: Okay, Ron, we're almost done here. So, here's your big chance: tell me your favorite joke.

RON: [A very long pause] Wow, that's really a tough question. I can't decide. So, let me give you two that I really, really like. The first one is a Jerry Seinfeld joke. It's very short, and yet it is very successful at gently poking fun at and shedding a little light on a rather sacred institution in our society—namely, marriage.

You know, I never knew that my voice had a tone, until I got married!

My second joke is not particularly novel, edifying, or edgy. In fact, it's rather formulaic, and the punch line can easily be changed to fit the demographics of any particular audience. But it's clever. It's funny. It makes me laugh.

And I keep telling it because, bottom line, isn't that what joke telling is supposed to do . . . make us laugh, make us feel good?

The Bronze Rat

A tourist wanders into a back-alley antiques shop in San Francisco's Chinatown. Picking through the objects on display, he discovers a detailed, life-sized bronze sculpture of a rat. The sculpture is so interesting and unique that he picks it up and asks the shop owner what it costs.

"Twelve dollars for the rat, sir," says the shop owner, "and a thousand dollars more for the story behind it."

"You can keep the story, old man," he replies, "but I'll take the rat."

The transaction complete, the tourist leaves the store with the bronze rat under his arm. As he crosses the street in front of the store, two live rats emerge from a sewer drain and fall into step behind him. Nervously looking over his shoulder, he begins to walk faster, but every time he passes another sewer drain, more rats come out and follow him. By the time he's walked two blocks, at least a hundred rats are at his heels, and people begin to point and shout. He walks even faster and soon breaks into a trot as multitudes of rats swarm from sewers, basements, vacant lots, and abandoned cars. Rats by the thousands are at his heels, and as he sees the waterfront at the bottom of the hill, he panics and starts to run full tilt.

No matter how fast he runs, the rats keep up, squealing hideously, now not just thousands but millions, so that by the time he comes rushing up to the water's edge, a trail of rats twelve city blocks long is behind him. Making a mighty leap, he jumps up onto a light post, grasping it with one arm while he hurls the bronze rat into San Francisco Bay with the other, as far as he can heave it. Pulling his legs up and clinging to the light post, he watches in amazement as the seething tide of rats surges over the breakwater into the sea, where they drown.

Shaken and mumbling, he makes his way back to the antiques shop.

"Ah, so you've come back to buy the story," says the owner.

"No," says the tourist. "But I was wondering if you have a bronze lawyer for sale?"

Let me add here, Al, that even this, my favorite joke, raises ethical questions. I'm the father of a lawyer. Some would say that jokes like this one foster disrespect for those in that profession. Nevertheless, I think this joke falls primarily on the side of just being funny.

AL: Thanks, Ron, for your hospitality and conversation. Allow me to end this session with the gift of a joke that I'm sure will reinforce your bias and dislike of sports.

Joe gets a ticket to the Super Bowl from his company, but when he gets there, his seat is in the last row in the corner of the stadium. Halfway through the first quarter, Joe sees through his binoculars an empty seat ten rows off the field, right on the fifty-yard line. He decides to take a chance and makes his way to the empty seat.

As he sits down, Joe says to the guy sitting next to him, "Excuse me, is anybody sitting here?"

The guy says, "No."

Joe says, "This is incredible! Who in their right mind would have a seat like this for the Super Bowl and not use it?"

The guy says, "Well, actually, the seat belongs to me. I was supposed to come with my wife, but she passed away. This is the first Super Bowl we haven't seen together since we got married in 1967."

Joe says, "That's really sad. But couldn't you find anyone to take the seat? A friend or a close relative?"

The guy says, "No, they're all at the funeral."

HATE SPEECH

Social theorist Arthur Koestler has argued that a consistent scornful and contemptuous style of humor is, in essence, contempt for all things unfamiliar and a "defensive antidote to sympathy." It can also be argued that the persistent pattern of derogatory humor is a demonstration of deep-seated aggression, fear, and rage. I couldn't agree more.[8]

I am convinced unethical jokes border on and are analogous to some aspects of hate speech. In our society, the First Amendment right to freedom of speech is a sacred concept in our democratically based form of constitutional government. However, our collective affirmation of the principle that "Congress shall make no law . . . abridging the freedom of speech, or of the press" is not an absolute. The courts have acknowledged that certain forms of speech, especially those that cause harm, are not protected by the First Amendment. Yelling "Fire!" in a crowded auditorium in the absence of fire is a classic example of an exception to the rule, and hate speech is another.

Hate speech is speech that attacks a person or group on the basis of gender, ethnic origin, race, disability, or sexual orientation. It is a form of speech that intends to disparage, humiliate, or intimidate an individual or group. It is a form of speech that may invite violence or prejudicial actions against an individual or group. Bottom line, freedom of speech does not mean the freedom to denigrate a person's sense of dignity, terrorize individuals, incite hatred, or encourage violence. Here's a rather horrifying and grotesque contemporary example of hate speech, which sadly has currency with a certain kind of audience:

Q: What do you call an open grave site filled with a hundred decapitated Muslims?
A: A good beginning!

Hate speech, like unethical jokes, stereotypes groups and individuals as stupid, dangerous, or impure. Unethical jokes, like hate speech, harm both individuals and society at large. Moreover, humor based on hate, prejudicial bias, and fear is rarely an invitation to dialogue and openness with others. The old childhood adage "Sticks and stones may break my bones, but words will never hurt me" is simply not true! Hate jokes undermine the public good and create animosity and distrust.

Like bullets, hate jokes destroy; they destroy the truest purpose of all humor and the comedic tradition. As journalist and critic Phil Berger succinctly put it, "What comics at every level try to do is to make something funny out of the everyday tumults of life."[9] Humor is an antidepressant. Humor, even dark humor, can offer insights, moments of lucidity, and a recognition of human potential. According to French philosopher André Comte-Sponville, humor is not an expression of hate, but rather an "expression of generosity." To make someone laugh is an act of kindness, an expression of care, concern, and respect, qualities directly opposite and contrary to the purpose and focus of hate jokes.[10]

My Uncle Joe was not the only person in my family to talk to me about the importance of being funny. *Mia nonna*, my grandmother, Uncle Joe's mama, was always telling jokes, which is perhaps where Uncle Joe picked up his lifelong habit. On more than one occasion she admonished me, "Alfredó, life is hard. Don't make it harder. Laugh and try to make other people laugh, too. But don't be cruel. Don't laugh at anyone. Laugh with them. Not at them!"

CHAPTER 6

Philogagging: Humor in the Classroom and Beyond

A serious and good philosophical work could be written consisting entirely of jokes.

—L. WITTGENSTEIN

I've been teaching philosophy as a required subject to class-rooms full of reluctant and unwilling students for more than four decades. Lately it's been harder and harder to get through to them. They seem to approach the class with "fear and loathing." You can see it in their eyes and the expressions on their faces:

"Why do I have to take this class?"

"What does it have to do with my major?"

They seem uninterested and unengaged. I want to expose them to the big philosophical questions in life. I want them to wrestle with issues of meaning, value, and purpose. They just want to pass the class.

The disconnect has been painful for me.

Having said this, my students do have a point! Studying philosophy is difficult and challenging. Philosophy tries to address the perennial and unavoidable questions and problems of life: Why am I? Who am I? What do I owe others? These kinds of questions are daunting, intimidating, and, at times, disheartening. Their possible resolutions are not easily captured in a simple syllogism or a straightforward Power-Point presentation. Moreover, the size and scope of these issues and questions often tend to blunt our interest and willingness to pursue them.

So, in the last couple of years I've been trying to pedagogically seduce my students into thinking philosophically by describing each course with a joke and lacing my lectures with jokes to keep them involved. I call it "enter-trainment." That is, if I can "entertain" them with a joke—if I can grab their attention and quicken their interest in what I'm saying—then maybe, just maybe, I can "train" them, or, more accurately, "educate" them, as well. But, just like any stand-up comic in a club, the jokes have to be funny or I'll lose my audience.

Although philosophy and joke telling do not share the same pedigree, with regard to many of the inescapable and impenetrable questions in life, both philosophy and joke telling do have an allied function and purpose. Philosophy, like joke telling, can help us to organize, interpret, possibly understand, or, at least, hopefully face and confront the fundamental issues of existence. Humor and joke telling can serve as a narrative playlet to metaphorically illuminate a complex philosophical concept. As I have argued earlier, joking about a deep topic or a dangerous topic is a way of talking about it, examining it in a way that doesn't scare us, numb us, and rob us of our joy in life. Jokes allow us to dwell on the incomprehensible without dying from fear or going mad. Laughter and joke telling are a way to speak of the unspeakable.[1] Humor gives us the courage to endure that which we cannot understand or avoid. Humor, like philosophy, prevents us from perceiving reality as a personal attack or a personal affront. In other words, humor allows us to wax philosophical, to theorize, to ponder life's mysteries.

Let me be a bit more precise about what I mean by using humor and jokes to teach philosophy: My purpose in the classroom is to be a teacher, not a comic. However, teaching, very much like being a stand-up comic, is a performance art, and teachers need to be engaging in order to capture their audience of students. However, every moment of every class should not simply be played for laughs and comedic effect. Rather, through the judicious use of joke telling, the instructor needs to create an atmosphere of "respectful playfulness" that allows students an opportunity to comfortably address some of the complexities and conundrums of the human condition. The purpose of joke telling in the classroom is not the joke, per se. Rather, humor and joke telling should be used as a gentler way of speaking and dealing with difficult truths.

Thomas Cathcart and Daniel Klein are two writers who agree with my general thesis. They met as undergraduate philosophy majors in the 1960s at Harvard. Over the next forty-odd years, Cathcart and Klein remained close friends, went about their lives, and continued to reflect on the intersection between philosophy and joke telling. Finally, fearing that death or dementia would overtake them, they put pen to paper and produced the profoundly funny and charming text *Plato and a Platypus Walk into a Bar: Understanding Philosophy through Jokes.*

Their thesis is elegantly simple and straightforward: "The construction and payoff of jokes and the construction and payoff of philosophical concepts are made out of the same stuff." They tease the mind in similar ways. That's because philosophy and jokes proceed from the same general impulse: to confound our sense of the way things are, to flip our world upside down, and to ferret out hidden, often uncomfortable, truths about life. What the philosopher calls an insight, the gagster calls a zinger or a punch line.[2]

Cathcart and Klein call their way of approaching the perennial problems of humankind *philogagging*—wisdom through joke telling. The authors believe that philosophy courses should not be taught simply through the reading of the great classical texts and rational argumentation. They are convinced that the great philosophical concepts can best be illuminated by telling jokes as a catalyst for creative reflection. And so they offer *Plato and a Platypus* as a possible curriculum guide for those professors who want to try a new tactical approach to teaching philosophy.

Drawing on Cathcart and Klein's insights and their rich storehouse of humor, I have put together a standard list of philosophy classes with examples of the kinds of "introductory jokes" that I think best reveal and exemplify the essential subject matter of the class in question. These jokes are not enough in themselves to unpack everything that will be handled in the class, but they are a good beginning. If nothing else, they act as an icebreaker, a way to overcome initial student apathy and disinterest.

Logic: The Art of Reasoning (Inductive Reasoning: Moving from a Particular to a General)

Sherlock Holmes and Dr. Watson are on a camping trip. In the middle of the night Holmes wakes up and gives Watson a nudge. "Watson," he says, "look up in the sky and tell me what you see."

"I see millions of stars, Holmes," says Watson.

"And what do you conclude from that, Watson?"

Watson thinks for a moment. "Well," he says, "astronomically, it tells me that there are millions of galaxies and potentially billions of planets. Astrologically, I observe that Saturn is in Leo. Homologically, I deduce that the time is approximately a quarter past three. Meteorologically, I suspect that we will have a beautiful day tomorrow. Theologically, I see that God is all powerful, and we are small and insignificant. Uh, what does it tell you, Holmes?"

"Watson, you idiot! Someone has stolen our tent!"[3]

Metaphysics: The Nature of Time and Reality (Martin Heidegger: *Being and Time*)

A woman is told by her doctor that she has six months to live. "Is there anything I can do?" she asks.

"Yes, there is," the doctor replies. "You could marry a tax accountant."

"How will that help my illness?" the woman asks.

"Oh, it won't help your illness," says the doctor, "but it will make the six months seem like an eternity!"[4]

Epistemology: The Theory of Knowledge (George Berkeley: *Esse est percipi* [To be is to be perceived])

Three women are in a locker room dressing to play racquetball when a man runs through wearing nothing but a bag over his head. The first woman looks at his penis and says, "Well, it's not my husband." The second woman says, "No, it isn't." The third woman says, "He's not even a member of this club."[5]

Ethics: Doing the Right Thing (Honesty and Truth Telling)

A man wins $100,000 in Las Vegas, and, not wanting anyone to know about it, he takes it home and buries it in his backyard. The next morning he goes out back and finds only an empty hole. He sees footprints leading to the house next door, which belongs to a deaf-mute, so he asks the professor down the street, who knows sign language, to help him confront his neighbor. The man takes his pistol, and he and the professor knock on the neighbor's door. When the neighbor answers, the man waves the pistol at him and says to the professor, "You tell this guy that if he doesn't give me back my $100,000, I'm going to kill him right now!" The professor conveys the message to the neighbor, who responds that he hid the money in his own backyard under the cherry tree. The professor turns to the man and says, "He refuses to tell you. He says he'd rather die first."[6]

Thanatology (The Study of Death and Dying)

A minister, a priest, and a rabbi die in a car crash. They go to Heaven for orientation. They are all asked, "When you are in your casket, and friends, family, and congregants are mourning over you, what would you like to hear them say?"

The minister says, "I would like to hear them say that I was a wonderful husband, a fine spiritual leader, and a great family man."

The priest says, "I would like to hear that I was a wonderful teacher and a servant of God who made a huge difference in people's lives."

The rabbi replies, "I would like to hear them say, 'Look, he's moving.'"[7]

Philosophy of Religion (Pluralism and Diversity)

A man arrives at the gates of Heaven. Saint Peter asks, "Religion?"

The man says "Methodist."

Saint Peter looks down his list and says, "Go to room twenty-eight, but be very quiet as you pass room eight."

Another man arrives at the gates of Heaven. "Religion?"

"Baptist."

"Go to room eighteen, but be very quiet as you pass room eight."

A third man arrives at the gates. "Religion?"

"Jewish."

"Go to room eleven, but be very quiet as you pass room eight."

The man says, "I can understand there being different rooms for different religions, but why must I be quiet when I pass room eight?"

Saint Peter says, "The Jehovah's Witnesses are in room eight, and they think they're the only ones here."[8]

Philosophy of Human Nature (Ultimate Wisdom)

At a meeting of the college faculty, an angel suddenly appears and tells the head of the philosophy department, "I will grant you whichever of three blessings you choose: wisdom, beauty, or ten million dollars." Immediately, the professor chooses wisdom. There is a flash of lightning, and the professor appears transformed, but he just sits there, staring down at the table. One of his colleagues whispers, "Say something." The professor says, "I should have taken the money."[9]

"But seriously, ladies and gentlemen . . ." For all their joke telling, Cathcart and Klein are deadly earnest about arriving at "truth-through-humor." Both jokes and philosophy can challenge us to look at the world from a different perspective. Both jokes and philosophy can, using the words of the German Enlightenment philosopher Immanuel Kant—who, like his fellow philosopher, Friedrich Nietzsche, was not a particularly funny guy—jar us out of our "dogmatic slumber" and help us get a new or different perspective on our lives.

Come on—let's be honest: There are only three types of teachers whom you remember from your college or high school days. There were the bad ones whose complete lack of communication skills simultaneously bored you to death and made you angry as hell for wasting your time. Then there were the brilliant ones whose genius was self-evident and off the charts. Even if you could only follow along with about a third of what they had to say, you were fascinated by the show. And then there were the teachers and professors who regularly demonstrated a sense of humor in class. They weren't necessarily doing a stand-up routine, but they integrated humor into their presentations. They were the teachers who communicated a certain joy and pleasure in what they were doing. Even if you didn't care about the course, you cared about them and paid attention to what they had to say.

I very much like Cathcart and Klein's book, and I think its message should be used in the classroom. But, more important, I would make it required reading for junior and senior faculty members alike. Too often, in every academic field, we take ourselves far too seriously. Too often we get caught up in third levels of abstraction. Too often we use language and references that only similarly trained experts are privy to. We forget who our real audience is. We forget that we're supposed to be effective communicators and translators of important ideas to our students, not just our colleagues.

My argument for the use of jokes in the classroom is, I think, a further illustration of the central argument of this text: Humor is an "assault on the absurdity, perplexity, and incomprehensibility of life." Humor helps us reframe, recast, refocus, and reinterpret the mysteries and challenges of life. Humor allows us to unpack the taboos and poke fun at our limits, our fears, and our frailties. Joke telling allows us to deal with the undeniable, the unresolvable, and the unanswerable. Joke telling, like the study of philosophy, helps us to endure. Both joke telling and philosophy help us better negotiate reality.

However, there is an important caveat regarding joke telling in our lives. The dark side of my Uncle Joe's lifelong habit of "gently" opening a conversation with a joke is the practice of some individuals who boorishly bombard every conversation with jokes. Such individuals perfectly fulfill the dictionary definition of a buffoon: "a person given to course, excessive, undignified joking." Humor, to be effective, must be used wisely and well. The intentional and careful use of humor in the classroom, at home, at work, with family, and with friends can both inform and improve our lives. The judicious use of humor is fundamental to living a praiseworthy and flourishing life with others. But with too much joke telling, you wind up having the opposite effect.

The thesis of this book is somewhere between, on the one hand, the Pollyannaish optimism of Archbishop Desmond Tutu, who is convinced, despite all evidence to the contrary, that "the texture of our universe is one where there is no question at all but that goodness and laughter and justice will prevail,"[10] and, on the other hand, the maudlin fatalism expressed by the actor-clown Canio in Ruggero Leoncavallo's classic opera *Pagliacci*. In the aria "Vesti la giuba" (popularly known for its line "Ridi, Pagliaccio"), when Canio sings, "Laugh, clown, laugh," the implication is that although he makes others laugh, all the while his heart is breaking.[11]

My views are much more along the lines of the comedically astute, but not always politically and socially correct, Woody Allen: Humor is a coping mechanism. Humor acknowledges reality but acts as a buffer and attempts to neutralize our fear of it. As Allen succinctly put it, "My view of reality is that it's a grim place to be . . . but it's the only place that you can get good Chinese takeout!" For Allen, a sense of humor/joke telling provides a way of looking at the world and not being defeated by it. Like his comedic predecessor Charlie Chaplin, Allen believes that humor, laughter, joke telling allows us to "take our pain and play with it."[12]

Ted Cohen argues that jokes cannot be the entire human response to the great issues and challenges of life, but any response that does not include the possibility of joke telling is less than a totally and truly human response.[13] Humor, joke telling, and laughter are neither a cure nor a complete and sufficient answer to most of life's challenges and tragedies. But they are a necessary analgesic if we are to continue.

As I pointed out in the prologue, the time-honored purpose of comedy, comedians, and joke telling is to help us better negotiate reality. Humor can, but not always, make life more bearable and worthwhile.

Epilogue

I have tried . . . to be a philosopher, but . . . cheerfulness was always breaking in.

—Oliver Edwards

My steadfast belief is that humor is an attempt to deal with the palpable absurdity of life. Although humor cannot always resolve all of our dilemmas, questions, and terrors, it can ease the pain of our perplexities and allow us to carry on as best we can. Moreover, humor is fun and can lead to conviviality, community, and friendship. Because of this, I believe that we have an obligation (or Comedic Imperative) to personally practice and share the benefits of humor, laughter, and comedy with others.

Given the subject matter and focus of this book, I think it only fitting and proper to end with a few jokes. Although I regularly fall in and out of love with jokes that I hear and come upon, there is one joke that has remained my favorite for over thirty-five years. It was told to me by one of my longtime handball buddies, Larry Olive. Larry has spent his life playing the role of the charming, sarcastic, witty, tongue-in-cheek misanthrope-curmudgeon. And he has been very successful at it. Like my Uncle Joe, Larry always has a new joke to tell me, but I think this one should be enshrined in the Joke Hall of Fame. (By the way, Larry always tells this joke in a thick

Yiddish accent. According to him, it's not strictly necessary, "but it couldn't hurt!")

Sid and Izzi have been friends since childhood. They went to grammar school and high school together. They were roommates in college and after graduation started a business together. They married twin sisters and were each other's best man. They bought homes next door to each other, and their kids grew up together. Both were married for forty-five years, and their wives died within a year of each other.

To save a little money and to offer each other a little company, they moved in together. Recognizing that neither one of them would live forever, and curious about the afterlife, they made a pact: whoever died first should call right away and tell the other guy what it's like.

A year later, Sid dies, and Izzi dutifully buries him, sits shivah, and patiently waits by the phone for his call. The first night, nothing. The first week, nothing. The first year, nothing. And, sadly, Izzi gives up all hope of hearing from his lifelong friend again.

Two years later, at three in the morning, the phone rings. Surprised and confused, Izzi picks up the phone.

"Hello," says a familiar voice, "Izzi, it's me, Sid."

"You son of a bitch," says Izzi, "you don't call for years and now you call me at 3 o'clock in the morning! What kind of friend are you?"

"All right already," says Sid. "Hold on to your horses. This is the first chance I got to give you a call."

"So you say!" says Izzi. "But let's cut to the chase: So, tell me, how is it there? What's it like to be in Heaven?"

"Well," says Sid, "It's really kind of hard to explain."

"Fair enough," says Izzi. "Just start by telling me what you did today."

"Well, to tell you the truth," says Sid, "today was a perfect day . . . blue skies and beautiful mountains in the background. So, after a big breakfast, I made love a couple of times, took a walk, and had a nap. When I woke up, I had a light lunch, made love three or four times. Later in the afternoon, me and a couple of the other guys walked down to this gigantic waterfall area to have dinner. After a wonderful all-you-can-eat dinner, two of the ladies got the hots for me, and we had a three-way going for almost two hours. I was so exhausted that I fell asleep on the spot. When I woke up in the middle of the night looking for a snack and something to drink, I saw a pay phone nearby, and so I called you!"

"Oh, my God," says Izzi. "What a day! What a day! Heaven sounds fabulous! Heaven sounds perfect!"

"Heaven, Schmeven," snorts Sid. "I'm a buffalo in Wyoming!"

And speaking of prize-winning jokes, the *Chicago Tribune* once nominated the following as the "Best Bar Joke."[1]

Once a couple had the great misfortune to have born unto them a child whose body was incomplete. In fact, there was nothing to the unfortunate child but a head. But the couple did not despair, and they devoted themselves to rearing their bodiless child, and indeed they succeeded. Year after year they took care of the child and his special needs until finally his twenty-first birthday arrived. To celebrate, they took the child-head with them to their customary neighborhood bar, where they placed the head on the bar between them, and then the husband announced, "Today my son is twenty-one years old, and we're celebrating. Drinks for everyone!"

When the bartender had served everyone in the room and everyone had sung "Happy Birthday," the mother carefully poured her son's drink into his mouth, and then, to everyone's astonishment, suddenly the boy began to grow, and in a minute he had developed a full torso, complete with arms and hands.

"It's wonderful," exclaimed the boy. "Mother, Father, look at me! I have arms and hands. Now I will buy a round of drinks to celebrate this great development."

The bartender served everyone again. This time the boy said, "Look, everyone, now I can handle my own drink," and he lifted his glass and poured its contents into his mouth. At that, he began to grow again, and this time legs and feet appeared, and now he was a fully normal young man. As soon as his new feet could touch the floor, he was off the bar stool, singing and prancing about the room, and saying he would buy another round of drinks. But before the next round could be served, the young man staggered and fell to the floor, dead.

Looking across the bar mournfully, the bartender observed, "He should have quit while he was a head."

Hopefully the "punch line" of this joke is not the "headline" that critics use in reviewing this book and its thesis: "He Should Have Stopped While He Was Ahead." Nevertheless, having said all that I have said, let me end with a recent quotation from the doyenne of naughty sexual domesticity, Erica Jong: "I'm thinking that if we have to see the world as a tragedy or a comedy, we might as well see it as a comedy. It's more fun."[2]

NOTES

PROLOGUE

1. Robert Trachtenberg, dir., *Mel Brooks: Make a Noise*, PBS documentary (*American Masters*), 2013.

2. William Lee Miller, *Lincoln's Virtues* (New York: Alfred A. Knopf, 2002).

3. Doris Kearns Goodwin, "Lincoln and Leadership," Loyola University Chicago, February 11, 2009.

4. Joshua Wolf Shenk, *Lincoln's Melancholy: How Depression Challenged a President and Fueled His Greatness* (New York/Boston: Mariner Books, 2005), 182.

5. Ibid., 116.

6. Ibid.

7. Mark Twain, *Mark Twain on Common Sense* (New York: Skyhorse Publishing, 2014), 54.

8. Ricki Stern and Anne Sundberg, dirs., *Joan Rivers: A Piece of Work*, IFC Films, 2010, DVD.

9. Don Steinberg, ed., *Jokes Every Man Should Know* (Philadelphia: Quirk Books, 2008), 94, 95. This joke is a mutated version of one originally written and performed by the comedian Emo Philips in his comedy album, $E = MO2$, recorded live at Carolines on Broadway in New York City in 1985. Variations on this "classic joke" can now be found in numerous joke anthologies and books on humor.

10. Dorothy Parker, *The Collected Dorothy Parker* (London: Penguin Books, 1977), 79.

Chapter 1: A Brief, Highly Selective, and Somewhat Fallacious History of Humor and Joke Telling

1. Paul Johnson, *Humorists: From Hogarth to Noël Coward* (New York: HarperCollins, 2010), vii.

2. Ibid., viii.

3. Jim Holt, *Stop Me If You've Heard This: A History and Philosophy of Jokes* (New York: W. W. Norton, 2008), 8, 10.

4. Mary Beard, *Laughter in Ancient Rome: On Joking, Tickling, and Cracking Up* (Berkeley: University of California Press, 2014), 185, 186.

5. Jon Macks, *How to Be Funny* (New York: Simon and Schuster, 2003), 6.

6. Henry Beard, *X-Treme Latin: Unleash Your Inner Gladiator* (New York: Gotham Books, 2004), 8, 9.

7. Holt, *Stop Me If You've Heard This*, 15, 18, 22.

8. Joshua Wolf Shenk, *Lincoln's Melancholy: How Depression Challenged a President and Fueled His Greatness* (New York/Boston: Mariner Books, 2005), 181.

9. Beatrice K. Otto, *Fools Are Everywhere: The Court Jester Around the World* (Chicago: University of Chicago Press, 2001).

10. Ibid., 1.

11. Ibid.,102.

12. Ibid., 43.

13. Ibid., chapter 2.

14. Ibid., 31.

15. Paul Provenza and Dan Dion, *Satiristas: Comedians, Contrarians, Raconteurs and Vulgarians* (New York: It Books, 2010), xii, xiii, xix, xx.

16. Provenza would agree with Lady Mary Wortley Montagu, who once wrote, "Satire should, like a polished razor keen, / wound

with a touch that's scarcely felt or seen. Thine is an oyster knife, that hacks and hews; / The rage but not the talent to abuse." *To the Imitator of the First Satire of Horace*, book ii (1733).

17. Provenza and Dior, *Satiristas*, 10.

18. Ibid., 279.

19. Groucho Marx, *Groucho and Me* (New York: First Da Capo Press, 1959), 32.

20. Don Steinbery, "No Joke: Comics Now Pack Giant Stadiums," *Wall Street Journal*, Arena Section, August 28, 2015, D1. See also Molly Eichel, "Philly's Kevin Hart Packs the Linc on Biggest Comedy Tour Ever," Entertainment, *Philadelphia Inquirer*, updated August 23, 2015, http://www.philly.com/philly/entertain ment/20150823_Philly_s_Kevin_Hart_packs_the_Linc_on_big gest_comedy_tour_ever.html.

21. Warren St. John, "Seriously, the Joke Is Dead," Fashion and Style, *New York Times*, May 22, 2005, http://www.nytimes .com/2005/05/22/fashion/sundaystyles/seriously-the-joke-is -dead.html.

22. Gregory Cowles, Inside the List, *New York Times*, July 5, 2015, 26, found in a slightly modified version online as "Sparks and Recreation," at http://www.nytimes.com/2015/07/05/books/ review/inside-the-list.html.

23. Zach Freeman, "Louis C.K. Is Master of His Domain at Chicago Theatre," Arts and Entertainment, *Chicago Tribune*, June 2, 2016, http://www.chicagotribune.com/entertainment/theater/com edy/ct-louis-ck-chicago-theatre-ent-0603-20160602-story.html.

24. Ibid.

25. Ibid.

26. *A Prairie Home Companion: Pretty Good Joke Book*, 6th ed. (Minneapolis: HighBridge, 2015), 7, 8, 9.

CHAPTER 2: HOW DO YOU MAKE FUNNY? SO, WHAT'S A JOKE?

1. Jim Holt, *Stop Me If You've Heard This: A History and Philosophy of Jokes* (New York: W. W. Norton, 2008), 48, 49.

2. Scott Weems, *Ha! The Science of When We Laugh and Why* (New York: Basic Books, 2014), 23.

3. F. H. Buckley, *The Morality of Laughter* (Ann Arbor: University of Michigan Press, 2005), 23.

4. John Morreall, ed., *The Philosophy of Laughter and Humor* (New York: State University of New York Press, 1987), 112.

5. Ibid., 112–16.

6. Bob Mankoff, *How about Never—Is Never Good for You? My Life in Cartoons* (New York: Henry Holt, 2014), 4.

7. Simon Critchley, *On Humour* (London: Routledge, 2004), 1.

8. Ted Cohen, *Jokes: Philosophical Thoughts on Joking Matters* (Chicago: University of Chicago Press, 1999), 4, 9, 10, 11.

9. Peter McGraw and Joel Warner, *The Humor Code: A Global Search for What Makes Things Funny* (New York: Simon and Schuster, 2014), 114.

10. Ibid., 115.

11. Dave Schwensen, *How to Be a Working Comic: An Insider's Guide to a Career in Stand-Up Comedy* (New York: Back Stage Books, 1998), 12.

12. Critchley, *On Humour*, 6, 7.

13. David Brenner, *I Think There's a Terrorist in My Soup: How to Survive Personal and World Problems with Laughter—Seriously* (Kansas City, MO: Andrews McMeel, 2003), xvii.

14. For more on the reaction to Gilbert Gottfried's tweets, see Shari Weiss and Cristina Everett, "50 Cent, Gilbert Gottfried Under Fire for Joking about Japan Earthquake, Tsunami," *New York Daily News*, March 14, 2011, http://www.nydailynews.com/enter

tainment/gossip/50-cent-gilbert-gottfried-fire-joking-japan-earth
quake-tsunami-article-1.117707.

15. Mark Twain said, "Never leave a funeral without telling
a joke and sharing a laugh about the deceased." About.com, s.v.
"Mark Twain Quotes," http://politicalhumor.about.com/od/funny
quotes/a/Mark-Twain-Quotes.htm.

16. Cohen, *Jokes*, 12, 26, 27.

17. Lewis Black, *History of the Joke, with Lewis Black*, DVD,
History Channel, produced by Marc Etkind, May 9, 2008.

18. Andrew Hudgins, *The Joker: A Memoir* (New York:
Simon and Schuster, 2013), xii.

19. Cohen, *Jokes*, 26, 27.

20. Steven Martin, *Born Standing Up: A Comic's Life* (New
York: Scribner, 2007), 1.

CHAPTER 3: COMEDY AND COPING WITH REALITY

1. Ted Cohen, *Jokes: Philosophical Thoughts on Joking Matters* (Chicago: University of Chicago Press, 1999), 1.

2. Jason Gay, "Robin Williams and Dario Pegoretti: The
Comedian and the Bike Builder," *Wall Street Journal*, updated
August 14, 2014, http://www.wsj.com/articles/robin-williams-and
-dario-pegoretti-the-comedian-and-the-bike-builder-1407970079.

3. Al Gini, John Powers, and Aaron Freeman, "One Flight
Up," *Humor and Stand-Up Comedy*, WBEZ, 91.5 FM, Chicago
Public Radio, May 6, 1992.

4. Carl Reiner, *I Remember Me* (Bloomington, IN: Author-
House, 2013), viii.

5. Andrew Hudgins, *The Joker: A Memoir* (New York: Simon
and Schuster, 2013), 50.

6. Cohen, *Jokes*, xi, 25, 50, 29.

7. Victor Borge and Robert Sherman, *My Favorite Intermissions: Victor Borge's Lives of the Musical Greats and Other Facts*

You Never Knew You Were Missing, illustrated by Thomas Winding (Garden City, NY: Doubleday, 1971), 140.

8. See Paul E. McGhee, *Health, Healing, and the Amuse System: Humor as Survival Training,* 3rd ed. (Dubuque, IA: Kendall/Hunt, 1999), 225. See also John Morreall, *Humor Works* (Amherst, MA: HRD Press, 1997), 249. Slightly different versions of this letter/joke can be found in these two texts. Neither author offers any other source for this material. As is the case with so many jokes, they are created, used, altered, expanded on, and shared and eventually informally achieve the status of public domain.

9. Gina Barreca, "What's Sounny?" Features, *Ms.,* Summer 2004, http://www.msmagazine.com/summer2004/whatsfunny.asp.

10. Christopher Hitchens, "Why Women Aren't Funny," Christopher Hitchens (website), https://christopherhitchens.net/why-women-arent-funny. Originally published in *Vanity Fair,* January 1, 2007, http://www.vanityfair.com/culture/2007/01/hitchens200701.

11. Jeff Nilsson, "'If I Couldn't Tell These Stories, I Would Die': Lincoln and Laughter," *Saturday Evening Post,* March 27, 2010, http://www.saturdayeveningpost.com/2010/03/27/history/post-perspective/lincoln-laughter.html.

12. P. M. Zall, ed. and intro., *Abe Lincoln Laughing: Humorous Anecdotes from Original Sources by and about Abraham Lincoln,* foreword by Ray Allen Billington (Knoxville: University of Tennessee Press, 1997), ix.

13. Ibid., ix, x.

14. Bob Dole, ed., *Great Presidential Wit: I Wish I Was in This Book* (New York: Scribner, 2001), 42.

15. Ibid., 47.

16. Paul Johnson, *Heroes: From Alexander the Great and Julius Caesar to Churchill and de Gaulle,* 1st ed. (New York: HarperCollins, 2007), 259.

17. Ibid., 258.

18. André Comte-Sponville, *A Small Treatise on the Great Virtues: The Uses of Philosophy in Everyday Life*, trans. Catherine Temerson (New York: Metropolitan Books, 2001), 217.

19. Christopher Buckley, "Booze as Muse," SundayReview, Opinion, *New York Times*, June 29, 2013, 5, http://www.nytimes .com/2013/06/30/opinion/sunday/booze-as-muse.html.

20. Arthur Koestler, *The Act of Creation* (New York: Arkana, 1989), 95.

21. Hudgins, *The Joker*, 102.

22. Ben Greenman, "Was It Something I Said?" review of *The Joker: A Memoir*, by Andrew Hudgins, *New York Times*, July 5, 2013, 13, Sunday Book Review, http://www.nytimes.com/2013/07/07/ books/review/the-joker-a-memoir-by-andrew-hudgins.html.

23. Joan Didion, "After Life," *New York Times Magazine*, September 25, 2005, http://www.nytimes.com/2005/09/25/magazine/ after-life.html.

24. Eugen Fink, *Nietzsche's Philosophy*, trans. Goetz Richter (New York: Continuum, 2003), 157.

25. Comte-Sponville, *A Small Treatise on the Great Virtues*, 217.

26. Ibid., 221.

27. Cohen, *Jokes*, 44, 45.

28. Ricki Stern and Anne Sundberg, dirs., *Joan Rivers: A Piece of Work*, IFC Films, 2010, DVD.

29. Mark Twain, *Mark Twain: The Mysterious Stranger, and Other Curious Tales* (New York: Gramercy Books, 1997), 97.

30. Joke as told by Denis Leary.

31. Andrew Hudgins, "The Joke's On All of Us," SundayReview, Opinion, *New York Times*, June 8, 2013, 8, http://www.nytimes .com/2013/06/09/opinion/sunday/the-jokes-on-all-of-us.html.

32. Robert R. Provine, *Laughter: A Scientific Investigation* (New York: Viking, 2000).

33. Samuel Taylor Coleridge, *The Complete Poetical Works of Samuel Taylor Coleridge, Including Poems and Versions of Poems Now Published for the First Time*, edited, with textual and bibliographical notes, by Ernest Hartley Coleridge (Oxford: Clarendon, 1912), 481.

CHAPTER 4: DIRTY JOKES, TASTELESS JOKES, ETHNIC JOKES

* Epigraph courtesy of "The Limerick," *Princeton Tiger*, November 1902, 59. A version of this chapter first appeared as Al Gini, "Dirty Jokes, Tasteless Jokes, Ethnic Jokes," *Florida Philosophical Review* 15, no. 1 (Winter 2015), http://philosophy.cah.ucf.edu/fpr/files/15_1/Gini.pdf.

1. David Galef, "What's Not Funny," *Common Review* 2, no. 1 (Winter 2002): 24.

2. Ibid., 22.

3. Ibid., 22, 26.

4. Mark C. Weeks, "Laughter, Desire, and Time," *Humor* 15, no. 4 (November 2002): 383–400.

5. Ruth Tallman, "Go F*** Yourself: The Aesthetic Evaluation of Offensive Humor," with Landon Schurtz, Society of Lighthearted Philosophers Conference, Tampa, Florida, October 15–16, 2010.

6. Ted Cohen, *Jokes: Philosophical Thoughts on Joking Matters* (Chicago: University of Chicago Press, 1999), 83.

7. Ibid., 85–87.

8. Adam Sternbergh, "Jeff Garlin Is the Funniest Guy in the Room. Except for Larry David," Talk, *New York Times Magazine*, July 17, 2013, http://www.nytimes.com/2013/07/21/magazine/jeff-garlin-is-the-funniest-guy-in-the-room-except-for-larry-david.html.

9. Chris Jones, "Why Seinfeld Took a Stand Against Political Correctness," Arts and Entertainment, *Chicago Tribune*, Section 4, June 12, 2015, 4, http://www.chicagotribune .com/entertainment/theater/comedy/ct-seinfeld-political-correct ness-column.html.

10. G. Legman, *Rationale of the Dirty Joke: An Analysis of Dirty Humor* (New York: Simon and Schuster Paperback, 1996).

11. Carlin's original routine reproduced in Justin R. Erenkrantz, "George Carlin's Seven Dirty Words," Justin R. Erenkrantz (website), last modified August 20, 2010, http://www.erenkrantz .com/Humor/SevenDirtyWords.shtml. See also Jacques Steinberg, "Refusing to Coast on 7 Infamous Words," Television, *New York Times*, November 4, 2005, http://www.nytimes.com/2005/11/04/ arts/television/refusing-to-coast-on-7-infamous-words.html.

12. Barry Dougherty, ed., *The Friars Club: 2069 Rather Naughty Jokes* (New York: Tess Press, 2010), 10.

13. Ibid., 403.

14. Ibid., 10.

15. Ibid., 251.

16. David Denby, "Dirty Business: 'Pretty Persuasion' and 'The Aristocrats,'" *New Yorker*, August 29, 2005, 92, http://www. newyorker.com/magazine/2005/08/29/dirty-business.

17. Mark Sinclair, "Tangled Up in Blue," *Time Out Chicago*, no. 24, August 29, 2005, 12. Although this joke can be found numerous places in print—as well as the approximately one hundred versions offered in the documentary *The Aristocrats* (Penn Jillette and Paul Provenza, dirs., THINKFilm, 2005)—the version I have selected seems the clearest and most logically organized for our needs.

18. Simon Critchley, *On Humour* (London: Routledge, 2004), 69.

19. Charles Leroux, "Humor in the Heartland: Tracking the Sociology of Ethnic Jokes," *Chicago Tribune*, Section 5, January

8, 2004, 1, 8, 13, http://articles.chicagotribune.com/2004-01-08/features/0401080289_1_scandinavian-norwegian-jokes.

20. Sam Hoffman, *Old Jews Telling Jokes: 5,000 Years of Funny Bits and Not-So-Kosher Laughs*, with Eric Spiegelman (New York: Villard Books, 2010).

21. Viktor Frankl, *Man's Search for Meaning: An Introduction to Logotherapy* (New York: Pocket Books, 1963), xi.

22. Viktor Frankl, *Man's Search for Meaning*, part 1 translated by Ilse Lasch, foreword by Harld S. Kushner, afterword by William J. Winslade (Boston: Beacon Press, 2006), x.

23. Paul E. McGhee, *Health, Healing and the Amuse System: Humor as Survival Training*, 3rd ed. (Dubuque, IA: Kendall/Hunt, 1999), 20.

24. Ibid., 81.

25. Paul E. McGhee, "Using Humor to Cope: Humor in Concentration/POW Camps," The Laughter Remedy (website), n.d., http://www.laughterremedy.com/article_pdfs/Using%20Humor%20to%20Cope-Part%202.pdf.

26. Rudolph Herzog, *Dead Funny: Telling Jokes in Hitler's Germany*, trans. Jefferson Chase (New York: Melville House, 2012), 6.

27. Ibid., 210.

28. Ibid., 5.

29. Cohen, *Jokes*, 63, 64, 65.

30. Critchley, *On Humour*, 65.

CHAPTER 5: A CONVERSATION WITH A COLLEAGUE ABOUT HUMOR AND ETHICS

1. Monica Heisey, "Amy Schumer: Comedy's Viral Queen," *Guardian*, June 28, 2015, http://www.theguardian.com/tv-and-radio/2015/jun/28/amy-schumer-comedys-viral-queen.

2. Ibid.

3. A. O. Scott, "Adjusting to a World that Won't Laugh with You," Cross Cuts, *New York Times*, June 5, 2015, https://www.nytimes.com/2015/06/07/movies/adjusting-to-a-world-that-wont-laugh-with-you.html.

4. F. H. Buckley, *The Morality of Laughter* (Ann Arbor: University of Michigan Press, 2005), 7.

5. Allen Salkin, "Comedy on the Hot Seat," Fashion and Style, *New York Times*, December 3, 2006, 1, 6, http://www.nytimes.com/2006/12/03/fashion/03comedy.html.

6. Al Gini, *Why It's Hard to Be Good* (New York: Routledge, 2006), 1.

7. James Martin, *Between Heaven and Mirth: Why Joy, Humor, and Laughter Are at the Heart of the Spiritual Life*, 1st ed. (New York: HarperOne, 2011), 108.

8. Arthur Koestler, *The Act of Creation* (New York: Arkana, 1989), 53.

9. Phil Berger, *The Last Laugh: The World of Stand-Up Comics* (New York: Cooper Square Press, 2000), 458.

10. André Comte-Sponville, *A Small Treatise on the Great Virtues: The Uses of Philosophy in Everyday Life*, trans. Catherine Temerson (New York: Metropolitan Books, 2001), 217.

CHAPTER 6: PHILOGAGGING: HUMOR IN THE CLASSROOM AND BEYOND

A version of this chapter first appeared as Al Gini, "The Importance of Humor in Teaching Philosophy," *Teaching Philosophy* 34, no. 2 (June 2011): 143–149.

1. Ted Cohen, *Jokes: Philosophical Thoughts on Joking Matters* (Chicago: University of Chicago Press, 1999), 45.

2. Thomas Cathcart and Daniel Klein, *Plato and a Platypus Walk into a Bar: Understanding Philosophy through Jokes* (New York: Abrams Image, 2006), 2.

3. Ibid., 30, 31.

4. Ibid., 20.

5. Ibid., 59.

6. Ibid., 149.

7. The thanatology class and its introductory joke are not found in *Plato and a Platypus*; I took the liberty of adding the class and the joke.

8. Cathcart and Klein, *Plato and a Platypus*, 106, 107.

9. Ibid., 79.

10. Alex Perry, "The Laughing Bishop," *Time*, October 11, 2010, 60, http://content.time.com/time/magazine/article/0,9171,2022647,00.html.

11. A synopsis of Ruggiero Leoncavallo's 1892 opera, *Pagliacci* (The Clowns), can be found at "'I Pagliacci': Synopsis," Music with Ease (website), n.d., http://www.musicwithease.com/pagliacci-synopsis.html.

12. Eric Lax, *Conversations with Woody Allen: His Films, the Movies, and Moviemaking* (New York: Alfred A. Knopf, 2009).

13. Cohen, *Jokes*, 40, 41.

Epilogue

1. Allan Johnson, "A Great One Is Worth $1,000," *Chicago Tribune*, Section 13, August 7, 2005, 9, http://articles.chicagotribune.com/2005-08-07/features/0508070426_1_dead-son-drink-boy.

2. Erica Jong, *Fear of Dying*, 1st ed. (New York: St. Martin's Press, 2015), 50.

Suggested Readings/
Humor and Comedy

Academically Focused Books

Beard, Mary. *Laughter in Ancient Rome: On Joking, Tickling, and Cracking Up*. Berkeley: University of California Press, 2014.

Berger, Phil. *The Last Laugh: The World of Stand-Up Comics*. New York: Cooper Square Press, 2000.

Buckley, F. H. *The Morality of Laughter*. Ann Arbor: University of Michigan Press, 2005.

Capps, Donald. *A Time to Laugh*. New York: Continuum, 2005.

Cohen, Ted. *Jokes: Philosophical Thoughts on Joking Matters*. Chicago: University of Chicago Press, 1999.

Critchley, Simon. *On Humour*. London: Routledge, 2004.

Errett, Benjamin. *Elements of Wit*. New York: Perigee, 2014.

Herzog, Rudolph. *Dead Funny: Telling Jokes in Hitler's Germany*. Translated by Jefferson Chase. New York: Melville House, 2012.

Holt, Jim. *Stop Me If You've Heard This: A History and Philosophy of Jokes*. New York: W. W. Norton, 2008.

Hudgins, Andrew. *The Joker: A Memoir*. New York: Simon and Schuster, 2013.

Johnson, Paul. *Humorists: From Hogarth to Noël Coward*. New York: HarperCollins, 2010.

Jonas, Peter M. *Secrets of Connecting Leadership and Learning with Humor*. Lanham, MD: Scarecrow Education, 2004.

Kaplan, Eric. *Does Santa Exist?* New York: Dutton, 2014.

Martin, James, S.J. *Between Heaven and Mirth: Why Joy, Humor, and Laughter Are at the Heart of the Spiritual Life*. New York: HarperOne, 2011.

McGraw, Peter, and Joel Warner. *The Humor Code: A Global Search for What Makes Things Funny*. New York: Simon and Schuster, 2014.

Morreall, John. *Comedy, Tragedy, and Religion*. Albany: University of New York Press, 1999.

Nesteroff, Kliph. *The Comedians: Drunks, Thieves, Scoundrels, and the History of American Comedy*. New York: Grove Press, 2015.

Otto, Beatrice K. *Fools Are Everywhere: The Court Jester Around the World*. Chicago: University of Chicago Press, 2001.

Provine, Robert R. *Laughter: A Scientific Investigation*. New York: Viking, 2000.

Trumble, Angus. *A Brief History of the Smile*. New York: Basic Books, 2004.

Weems, Scott. *Ha! The Science of When We Laugh and Why*. New York: Basic Books, 2014.

Zoglin, Richard. *Comedy at the Edge: How Stand-Up in the 1970s Changed America*. New York: Bloomsbury, 2008.

AUTOBIOGRAPHIES/BIOGRAPHIES

Allen, Steve. *Reflections*. Amherst, NY: Prometheus Books, 1994.

Ansari, Aziz, with Eric Klenenberg. *Modern Romance*. New York: Penguin, 2015.

Berle, Milton. *Milton Berle: An Autobiography*. New York: Applause Books, 2002.

Brosh, Allie. *Hyperbole and a Half*. New York: Simon and Schuster, 2013.

Bushkin, Henry. *Johnny Carson*. Boston: Eamon Dolan/Houghton Mifflin Harcourt, 2013.

Cho, Margaret. *I Have Chosen to Stay and Fight*. New York: Riverbend Books, 2005.

Cleese, John. *So, Anyway . . .* London: Random House, 2014.

Crystal, Billy. *Still Foolin' 'Em.* New York: Henry Holt, 2013.

Epstein, Lawrence J. *George Burns: An American Life.* Jefferson, NC: McFarland, 2011.

Fey, Tina. *Bossypants.* New York: Little, Brown, 2013.

Griggs, Jeff. *Guru: My Days with Del Close.* Lanham, MD: Ivan R. Dee, 2005.

Herbert, Emily. *Robin Williams: When the Laughter Stops, 1951–2014.* London: John Blake, 2014.

Knoedelseder, William. *I'm Dying Up Here: Heartbreak and High Times in Stand-Up Comedy's Golden Era.* New York: Public Affairs, 2009.

Kohen, Yael. *We Killed: The Rise of Women in American Comedy.* New York: Picador, 2013.

Maron, Marc. *Attempting Normal.* New York: Spiegel & Grau, 2013.

Martin, Steven. *Born Standing Up: A Comic's Life.* New York: Scribner, 2007.

Offerman, Nick. *Gumption.* New York: Dutton, 2015.

Poehler, Amy. *Yes Please.* New York: Dey Street/Morrow, 2015.

Quinn, Colin. *The Coloring Book.* New York: Grand Central, 2015.

Reiner, Carl. *I Remember Me.* Bloomington, IN: Author-House, 2013.

Rivers, Joan. *Diary of a Mad Diva.* New York: Berkley Books, 2014.

Rivers, Joan. *I Hate Everyone . . . Starting with Me.* New York: Berkley Books, 2012.

Rivers, Melissa. *The Book of Joan.* New York: Crown Archetype, 2015.

Schumer, Amy. *The Girl with the Lower Back Tattoo.* New York: Simon and Schuster, 2016.

Siegel, Lee. *Groucho Marx: The Comedy of Existence.* New Haven, CT: Yale University Press, 2015.

Wentworth, Ali. *Happily Ali After*. New York: Harper, 2015.

Zoglin, Richard. *Hope: Entertainer of the Century*. New York: Simon and Schuster, 2014.

Jokes, Joking, and Philosophy

Cathcart, Thomas. *The Trolley Problem*. New York: Workman, 2013.

Cathcart, Thomas, and Daniel Klein. *Aristotle and an Aardvark Go to Washington: Understanding Political Doublespeak through Philosophy and Jokes*. New York: Abrams Image, 2007.

Cathcart, Thomas, and Daniel Klein. *Heidegger and a Hippo Walk through Those Pearly Gates*. New York: Penguin, 2009.

Cathcart, Thomas, and Daniel Klein. *Plato and a Platypus Walk into a Bar: Understanding Philosophy through Jokes*. New York: Abrams Image, 2006.

Klein, Daniel. *The Travels with Epicurus*. New York: Penguin, 2012.

Books of Jokes

Brown, Judy, ed. *Jokes to Go*. Kansas City, MO: Andrews McMeel, 2003.

Brown, Judy, ed. *Squeaky Clean Comedy*. Kansas City, MO: Andrews McMeel, 2005.

Dedopulos, Tim, ed. *The Best 500 Pub Jokes*. London: Carlton, 2009.

Dole, Bob, ed. *Great Presidential Wit: I Wish I Was in This Book*. New York: Scribner, 2001.

Dougherty, Barry, ed. *The Friars Club: 2069 Rather Naughty Jokes*. New York: Tess Press, 2010.

Hoffman, Sam, with Eric Spiegelman. *Old Jews Telling Jokes: 5,000 Years of Funny Bits and Not-So-Kosher Laughs*. New York: Villard Books, 2010.

Kamien, Maria, ed. *Great One Liners*. Platinum Press, 2010.

Keyes, Ralph, ed. *The Wit and Wisdom of Oscar Wilde*. New York: Gramercy Books, 1999.

Mankoff, Bob. *How about Never—Is Never Good For You? My Life in Cartoons*. New York: Henry Holt, 2014.

A Prairie Home Companion: Pretty Good Joke Book. 6th edition. Minneapolis: HighBridge, 2015.

Price, Steven, ed. *1001 Funniest Things Ever Said*. Guilford, CT: Lyons Press, 2006.

Sheridan, Tom, ed. *The Book of Catholic Jokes*, Skokie, IL: ACTA, 2008.

Sheridan, Tom, ed. *The Second Book of Catholic Jokes*. Chicago: ACTA, 2010.

Steinberg, Don, ed. *Jokes Every Man Should Know*. Philadelphia: Quirk Books, 2008.

Weitzman, Ilana, Eva Blank, Alison Benjamin, Rosanne Green, Lisa Sparks, and Mike Wright, eds. *Jokelopedia*. New York: Workman, 2000.

BOOKS OF INTERVIEW

Apatow, Judd. *Sick in the Head: Conversations about Life and Comedy*. New York: Random House, 2015.

Provenza, Paul, and Dan Dion. *Satiristas: Comedians, Contrarians, Raconteurs and Vulgarians*. New York: It Books, 2010.

Sacks, Mike. *Poking a Dead Frog: Conversations with Today's Top Comedy Writers*. New York: Penguin, 2014.

How to Do It Books

Besser, Matt, Ian Roberts, Matt Walsh, Joe Wengert, and David Kantrowitz. *The Upright Citizens Brigade Comedy Improvisation Manual.* New York: Comedy Council of Nicea, 2013.

Hoffman, Eric, and Gary Rudoren. *Comedy by the Numbers.* San Francisco: McSweeney's, 2007.

Macks, Jon. *How to Be Funny.* New York: Simon and Schuster, 2003.

Schwensen, Dave. *How to Be a Working Comic: An Insider's Guide to a Career in Stand-Up Comedy.* New York: Back Stage Books, 1998.

Schwensen, Dave. *Comedy FAQs and Answers: How the Stand-Up Biz Really Works.* New York: Allworth Press, 2005.

INDEX

academia, humor and, 109–10
Aflac Inc., 28
aging jokes, 53
Allen, Woody, 111
Alonzo, Cristela, 37
animal jokes, xii, 33, 70–71, 96–97
Ansari, Aziz, 14
"The Aristocrats" (joke), 66–69
Aristophanes, 3
Aristotle, 87
attitude, xix–xx
audience: offensive jokes and, 60–62; success of joke and, 28–30

Beard, Henry, 4
"Bear Hunting" (joke), 70–71
Bee, Samantha, 12
Berger, Phil, 100
Berkeley, George, 106
Berle, Milton, xxi, 7–8
Berra, Yogi, xix
Birth, Mario, 11
Black, Lewis, 30, 65
Borge, Victor, 42
Bracciolini, Poggio, 4
"The Bronze Rat" (joke), 96–97
Brooks, Mel, xi–xii, 25–26, 28, 85
Browne, Charles Farrar, 4
Buckley, Christopher, 48
Burns, George, 7–8
business jokes, 54–55

cable television, 12
Carlin, George, 64–65
Carter, Judy, 32

Cathcart, Thomas, 103–4, 109
Chaplin, Charlie, 111
character, humor and, xxiv, 55, 89–90
Chesterton, G. K., 22
Cicero, 22
clubs, 10–11
Cohen, Myron, 15
Cohen, Ted, 23, 29, 35, 61, 111
Colbert, Steven, 12
Coleridge, Samuel Taylor, 56
comedians/comics: bombing, 36; qualifications of, 25. *See also* stand-up comedians
Comedians in Cars Getting Coffee, 16
comedy. *See* humor
Comte-Sponville, André, 51, 100
contemptuous humor, 20, 93–94, 98
coping, humor and, xi, xiii, xv–xvi, 10, 37–56, 111
Cosby, Bill, 15, 63
Cousins, Norman, 89

The Daily Show, xiii, 12
Dangerfield, Rodney, 34
death jokes, xvi–xvii, xvii–xviii, 23–24, 52, 107
defense mechanism, humor as, 48–55, 110–11
defiance, humor and, 80–81
delight, humor and, 38–40
Didion, Joan, 49
dirty/tasteless jokes, 27, 57–83
diversity, 107–8
"Dog for Sale" (joke), xii
Dundes, Alan, 19

Edwards, Oliver, 113
Egypt, 1
elephant jokes, 33
epistemology, 106
ethics: humor and, 85–100;
    jokes on, 54–55, 106–7;
    nature of, 87–88
ethnic jokes, 71–83, 86
existential angst, 54

Facebook, 13
fools, 5–7
formulaic jokes, 32–34
Foxworthy, Jeff, 83
Frankl, Victor, 55, 78–79
Freeman, Aaron, 40
Freud, Sigmund, 21–22, 50
Full Frontal, 12

Gaffigan, Jim, 11
Galef, David, 57–59
Garlin, Jeff, 62
gender, and humor, 43–45
Genesis, book of, 2
"Genie in the Bottle" (joke), 70
Goodwin, Doris Kearns, xiv
Gottfried, Gilbert, 27–28
Green, Ronald M., 44, 90–97
Griswold, Frank, 88
groaners, 39

habits, and ethics, 88–89
Hanson, Todd, 9–10
Hart, Kevin, 11
hate speech, 98–100
Heidegger, Martin, 105
Heisenberg, Werner, xx
Herzog, Rudolph, 80–81
Hitchens, Christopher, 44–45
Hobbes, Thomas, 72

Hoffman, Sam, 75–76
Holocaust, 78–81
honesty, 106–7
Hope, Bob, 7–8
Horace, 7
Hudgins, Andrew, 35, 40–41, 49
humanity: folly and, 5; humor
    and, 9–10, 111–12
human nature, 108
humor: analysis of, issues with,
    xviii, xx–xxi, 19; benefits of,
    38–55; in classroom, 101–11;
    functions of, xi–xii, xiii, xx,
    10; golden age of, 10–12;
    history of, 1–17; importance
    of, xix–xx, 89–90; nature
    of, 19–36; need for, xi–xii;
    offensive jokes and, 57–83;
    versus oppression, 86–87,
    93–94; and sociology, 14

illness jokes, 54
The Importance of Being Earnest
    (Wilde), xix
Incongruity Theory, 21
inductive reasoning, 105
Instagram, 13
Internet, 13–14
Ionesco, Eugène, 79
Isaac, meaning of, 3

James, William, 50
jesters, 5–7
Jewish jokes, 3, 32, 75–81
Jillette, Penn, 66
Johnson, Paul, 1–2, 45, 47
jokebooks, 3–4
jokes: content of, and success,
    25–26; definitions of, xi,
    19–36; history of, 1–17;

online, 13; and philosophy, 104; provenance of, xxi; structure of, 30; types of, 30–35; world's funniest joke, 23–24
joke telling: as conditional, 29; elements of, 24–30, 25t, 59t. *See also* humor
Jones, Chris, 62–63
Jong, Erica, 117

Kant, Immanuel, 109
Keillor, Garrison, 16–17, 74–75
Key, Keegan-Michael, xi
Kilborn, Craig, 12
Klein, Daniel, 103–4, 109
knock-knock jokes, 32–33
knowledge, theory of, 106
Koestler, Arthur, 49, 98

language, profane, 64–66
Last Week Tonight, 12
lawyer jokes, 34, 96–97
Leary, James P., 74
Legman, Gershon, 63, 66
Leibowitz, Harold, 77–78
Leoncavallo, Ruggero, 111
Leopardi, Giacomo, 6–7
Lewis, Jerry, 37
Liber Facetiarum (Bracciolini), 4
The Life of Brian (Monty Python), 28
light bulb jokes, 33
limericks, 57
Lincoln, Abraham, xiii–xv, 45–47
Locke, David, 4
logic, 105
Louis C.K., 16, 93

Maher, Bill, 12
male bonding, humor and, 43–45
Mankoff, Bob, 22
marriage jokes, xvi–xvii, 8, 34, 35, 52, 75, 95
Martin, Steve, 36, 87
Marx, Groucho, 10, 28, 35
Melissus, 3
metaphysics, 105–6
Miller, William Lee, xiv
Montagu, Mary Wortley, 120n16
Monty Python, 28
morality. *See* ethics

narrative jokes, 32
Newell, Robert H., 4
New York Times, 14
Nietzsche, Friedrich, 50, 92, 109
The Nightly Show, 12
Noah, Trevor, 12
Nussbaum, Emily, 86

offensive jokes, 27, 57–83
Ole and Lena jokes, 74–75
Olive, Larry, 113–14
Oliver, John, 12
one-liners, 35
The Onion, 9
Otto, Beatrice K., 5–7

Pagliacci (Leoncavallo), 111
Parker, Dorothy, xviii–xix
Peele, Jordan, xi
perception, 106
Periscope, 13
philogagging, 101–11; definition of, 104
Philogelos, or Laughter-Lover, 3

philosophy: challenges of, 101–2; instruction, humor and, 101–11
pleasure, humor and, 38–40
pluralism, 107–8
podcasts, 13–14
political jokes, xv, 52
Pope, Alexander, 7
practical jokes, 16–17
The Producers (Brooks), 28
profane language, 64–66
Provenza, Paul, 7, 66
punch line, 9, 25, 30, 104

quickie jokes, 34

Reagan, Ronald, 47–48
reality: humor and, xi, xiii, xv–xvi, 10, 37–56, 92, 111–12; nature of, 105–6
Real Time with Bill Maher, 12
redneck jokes, 83
Reiner, Carl, 40
relationships, humor and, 40–48, 110–11
Relief Theory, 21–22
religion jokes, xvii–xviii, 2–3, 53–54, 107–8
Rivers, Joan, xv, 7–8, 51

Sagal, Peter, 12
satire, 7; nature of, 9–10, 120n16
Saturday Night Live, xix, 11–12
Schumer, Amy, 11, 85–86, 94
Schwensen, Dave, 24
Seinfeld, Jerry, 15–16, 62–63, 95
sex jokes, xvi–xvii, 2–3, 8, 32, 52, 63–64, 69–71, 75, 86, 106
shaggy dog jokes, 30–32, 42–43
Shaw, George Bernard, 28

social asset, humor as, 91–92
sociology, and humor, 14
speech, freedom of, 98–99
sports, 44, 97–98
stand-up comedians, 7, 10; online, 13–14; and pleasure, 39–40; venues for, 10–11
Stewart, Jon, xiii, 12
Superiority Theory, 20

tasteless jokes. *See* dirty/tasteless jokes
thanatology, 107
time, nature of, 105–6
timing, 26–28
truth telling, 106–7
Tutu, Desmond, 47–48, 111
Twain, Mark, xv, 28, 51, 123n15
Twitter, 13

uncertainty principle, xx

Vera; or, The Nihilists (Wilde), xix
Vine, 13
virtue, 89–91

Wait Wait . . . Don't Tell Me, 12
West, Mae, 35
White, E. B., 19
Wilde, Oscar, xix
Williams, Robin, 9, 39–40
Wilmore, Larry, 12
wisdom, 108
Wiseman, Richard, 23–24
Wittgenstein, L., 101

Youngman, Henny, 34
YouTube, 13

Zall, Paul, 46

ABOUT THE AUTHOR

Al Gini is professor of business ethics at the Quinlan School of Business at Loyola University Chicago. He is cofounder and longtime associate editor of *Business Ethics Quarterly*, the journal of the Society for Business Ethics. For more than twenty-seven years he was resident philosopher on National Public Radio's Chicago affiliate, WBEZ, and he can currently be heard on WGN/Tribune Radio. His books include *My Job, My Self: Work and the Creation of the Modern Individual*; *The Importance of Being Lazy: In Praise of Play, Leisure and Vacation*; *Why It's Hard to Be Good*; *Seeking the Truth of Things: Confessions of a (Catholic) Philosopher*; *The Ethics of Business: A Concise Introduction*, with Alexei Marcoux; and *Ten Virtues of Outstanding Leaders: Leadership and Character*, with Ronald M. Green.